A THEATRE IN MY MIND

A THEATRE IN MY MIND

THE INSIDE STORY OF AUSTRALIAN RADIO DRAMA

REG JAMES WITH **JAMES AITCHISON**

Copyright © 2015 Reg James with James Aitchison

Published by Vivid Publishing
P.O. Box 948, Fremantle
Western Australia 6959
www.vividpublishing.com.au

National Library of Australia Cataloguing-in-Publication data:
Creator: James, Reg, author.
Title: A Theatre in my Mind : The inside story of Australian radio drama /
          Reg James with James Aitchison.
ISBN: 9781925341348 (paperback)
Subjects: Radio plays, Australian--History. Radio broadcasting--Australia--History.
Other Creators/Contributors: Aitchison, Jim, author.
Dewey Number: 791.4470994

Photographs courtesy of Grace Gibson company archives, and from author's collection and sources. If a credit has been overlooked, apologies are offered, and upon notification any omission will be rectified at the first opportunity.

All rights reserved. No part of this publication may be reproduced, stored in a retrieval system or transmitted in any form or by any means, electronic, mechanical, photocopying, recording or otherwise, without the prior written permission of the copyright owner. The information, views, opinions and visuals expressed in this publication are solely those of the author and do not reflect those of the publisher. The publisher disclaims any liabilities or responsibilities whatsoever for any damages, libel or liabilities arising directly or indirectly from the contents of this publication.

This book is dedicated to Miss Grace Gibson, and the actors and writers who made her radio shows such a success throughout the English-speaking world.

Contents

Episode 1: "The Boy" 9

Episode 2: Counting Pennies 17

Episode 3: The Reg Johnston Years 31

Episode 4: The Big Shows 39

Episode 5: The Great Voices 55

Episode 6: Competitive Edge 69

Episode 7: Country Roads 90

Episode 8: A New Adventure — Marriage 99

Episode 9: Up, Up, and Away 106

Episode 10: Uncertain Times 114

Episode 11: The Napier Line 128

Episode 12: Down But Not Out 140

Episode 13: Unsung Heroes 149

Episode 14: Never Off The Air 159

Acknowledgements 174

Addendum: The Final Chapter 177

Episode 1
"The Boy"

LITTLE did I know when I walked down a dingy, black-and-white tiled corridor in Savoy House, 29 Bligh Street, Sydney that I was embarking on a journey that would last a lifetime. It was March 1946, I was 16, and looking for a job. I had started a course on advertising. Lintas, the advertising agency for Lever Brothers, had offered me a position as office boy and making the tea. As it seemed I would be pushing the tea trolley most of the day, I was not interested.

When I saw an ad in the *Sydney Morning Herald* — "Boy wanted at radio production company" — I applied and was called in for an interview.

Like most of my friends at that time, I was an avid radio listener. The first radio drama programme I listened to was *Inspector Scott of Scotland Yard* — on a neighbour's radio — back in 1932. It was a complete story told in quarter-hour episodes each week. George Edwards produced the show and played all the male characters. To this day I have never been able to learn whether they were recorded or just performed live in the studio. Another favourite of mine was *Yes, What?* Set in the classroom from Hell, I still think it was the funniest radio show of all time. The situations in every episode were the same; raucous schoolboys giving their teacher grief. Like a typical boy of that era, I could always relate to the things that happened. It proved to be a perennial hit just like my other favourite show of that era, *Dad and Dave*, not exactly a comedy show at the time it was written, but I got lots of laughs out of it. Those three shows were enshrined in my mind as all-time radio classics, perhaps because of my impressionable age at the time, and what impresses you as a child stays with you. I also enjoyed the Nyal plays. I knew the names of some of the actors, too — John Saul and Lyndall Barbour were famous — but when I applied for the job, I had no idea who Grace Gibson was.

I was ushered into this mysterious woman's office. I knew at once that in some way she was foreign. She was tall, dark-haired, and spoke with an accent that I did not quite understand. I could not quite put my finger on it. I thought she looked Spanish, because of her dark colouring and black hair, but she did not speak with a Spanish accent. Her gaze was impassive, and I felt as though she was examining me like I was a bug in a bottle.

I was completely overwhelmed in her presence. She made me talk about my family and that helped settle my nerves. Luckily I remembered to say that I had started an advertising course, and she told me that her husband Ronnie had commenced the same course. I think that helped my chances. Beyond that, I have no clear recollection of what we talked about. But when it was time to go, I just *knew* I wanted to work for her company!

A few anxious days passed before the postman arrived with a letter saying I could start work the following Monday. My duties would include Roneo-ing scripts, putting them together in sets for the actors, carrying big transcription discs to radio stations and advertising agencies, and running messages for all and sundry. I would also be taught sound effects, which struck me as pretty good! (Grace told the story for years that a very handsome boy had also applied for the position, and while she was very taken with him, she gave me the job because I was bigger and could carry more records.)

My starting salary was £1/15/6 per week. What Grace did not realise was that I had a birthday in May. When I turned 17, it went up to £2/5/-. She always groused that I was a bit tough on her because she had to give me a pay rise almost at once.

In those days, even the office boy wore a suit and tie to work, with a neatly folded handkerchief in the breast pocket. I loved the atmosphere and the people from the very first day. Grace had two offices at Savoy House, roughly the size of two large suburban lounge rooms. She had one, and the staff shared the other. And, by some strange coincidence, she employed two Betty's and, after I joined, two Reg's. Grace's secretary, Betty Gondolf, helped cut stencils for the scripts and booked the casts for recording. Betty Barnard, a part-timer and an old friend of Grace's who would later become manager, shared a desk with the full-time script typist, Loris Gunn. Director-writer-actor-narrator Reg Johnston worked from a third desk. Along one wall was a wooden cabinet where all the transcription discs were stored. It faced a cluttered worktable where I packed discs and did battle with a cranky hand-operated Roneo machine that printed out scripts. Not long after I joined I discovered that in Grace's filing cabinet was a bottle of gin, from which all the employees would indulge themselves once Grace had left the office on Friday afternoons. It was my first taste of gin.

Grace's office was across the hall. It had a better carpet and a large radiogram, and every Monday morning fresh flowers were brought in from a florist in Hunter Street. This was where she previewed her shows to radio station executives. It was Grace's habit to talk all the way through the programmes she played, just in case her guests did not like them. She was always superbly dressed; she loved good clothes, frocks in bright colours, and never wore slacks. Today they call it power dressing.

I was completely in awe of her, and at times even a little intimidated. I never addressed her as anything but "Miss Gibson", certainly not Grace! As was customary in those days, the office junior called all the female employees "Miss" too — Miss Gondolf, Miss Gunn, Miss Barnard. And, of course, Reg Johnston was Mr Johnston.

Office hours were 9 am to 5.30 pm, plus one Saturday morning in every three. Grace, never one to be hurried, only started signing her mail at 5.25 pm so it was nearly 6 pm when I finally got away. I think I was supposed to mail it from the GPO in Martin Place, but that was too far for me to walk, so I usually put it in a box on the corner of Hunter Street. Why not? The mail still got through!

Because I never wanted to go to school, my parents thought I would never last long at a job. They were quite afraid for me, but they need not have worried. When I started work for Grace Gibson, I was *always* there! I used to just work back on my own sometimes if I had to catch up. I was happy. And I always had something to listen to.

WHEN I started working for Grace, her company had been in business for about fifteen months. As the weeks and months went by, I learned exactly who Grace Gibson was.

Grace Isabel Gibson was born on 17 June 1905 in El Paso, Texas, the third of four children. El Paso was on the Mexican border so it was not surprising that Grace was the product of two cultures. Her father was rancher and taxi driver Calvin Newton Gibson, a member of the Ku Klux Klan. Her mother, Margaret Escobara, was born in Mexico City. Grace not only inherited Mexican ancestry from her mother, but also a passionate love of spicy Mexican cuisine. With her heavy-lidded brown eyes, Grace was the master of the Mexican standoff — her impassive stare could be quite daunting when a deal was being negotiated. It would be true to say that Grace shared some of her father's Klan beliefs, but they became modified in later years. We have her husband Ronnie to thank for that.

Grace had been brought up hard and knew the meaning of a dollar.

Working at a local bank did not satisfy the ambitious young Texan. Like thousands of other girls her age, Grace set her sights on Hollywood and a job at Central Casting. When the Radio Transcription Company of America opened its doors, it was one of the first studios to record radio dramas for syndication to stations around the United States. Grace was one of its first employees; she started there as errand girl, switchboard operator, and two-fingered typist. Before long, her magnetic personality landed her the job of auditioning and selling the company's programmes to potential sponsors.

Fast forward to December 1933. Alfred Edward Bennett, known to all as A. E. Bennett, managing director of Sydney radio station 2GB, arrived in Hollywood looking for programmes. The visionary Bennett had heard about the new transcription technology; he knew that it would make better business sense for Australian commercial stations to use transcriptions rather than rent expensive government landlines to cover the vast distances between them; transcription discs could be despatched by mail for a fraction of the cost. As fate would have it, 28-year-old Grace was assigned to sell him all the programmes that her company had — which she did. Then she took him to all the other companies and sold him their programmes too.

Bennett made a triumphant return to Sydney in 1934. His vision had proved correct. 2GB began broadcasting all the new American transcriptions to great success. There was no shortage of willing sponsors, and other stations wanted to buy them too. But Bennett was sharp enough to know this was only the tip of the iceberg; the question was, how to take the transcription project forward. His mind turned to Grace Gibson and he called Hollywood. "On loan" from her employer, Grace arrived in Australia for six months — and stayed a lifetime.

She became the first manager of Bennett's new company — in fact, she even named it — American Radio Transcription Agencies. Its cable address was ARTRANSA. Later, when the company recorded its own transcribed shows in Sydney, it called itself Artransa. Grace pioneered the local transcription business. She was earning £40 a week as she established the method of selling, scheduling, and distributing the transcription discs from one station to another across Australia. One newspaper at the time called her "The Highest Paid Woman in Australia".

Artransa was located in Savoy House, 29 Bligh Street, above the Savoy Theatre. The building also housed 2GB, the key station of the Macquarie Network; 2UE, the key station of the Major Network; as well as the Australian Record Company.

In 1941, Grace's destiny changed yet again.

At one of socialite Nola Dekyvere's Red Cross charity events, Grace sold a raffle ticket to the dashing Randell Robert Ronald M'Donell Parr. Tall, handsome, athletic, Ronnie Parr was armed with a charming British persona, even though he was Irish. Grace, the girl from El Paso, was smitten at once. Ronnie was two or three years older than Grace, down from Shanghai to join the Australian forces. He *was* the perfect gentleman, but definitely no prude, and their attraction was immediate. The full story of their romance appears in *Yes, Miss Gibson*.

With the head of Consolidated Press Frank Packer as best man, Grace married Warrant-Officer Ronnie Parr at the Registrar-General's office in 1944. They were the ultimate "Odd Couple": the suave, perfectly-groomed gentleman and the loud, ambitious Texan. That same week, Grace broke her contract with 2GB, walked out, and opened her own company. Grace Gibson Radio Productions was in business.

GRACE set up her company at Savoy House, right under the noses of 2GB, 2UE, Artransa, and the Australian Record Company. Her good friend Frank Packer was keen to back her, but wanted 51 per cent of the company. Grace wanted complete control of her destiny and readily accepted the "no strings" deal offered by another powerful friend, advertising mogul Sim Rubensohn. He provided an interest-free financial agreement and set about obtaining sponsors to protect his investment.

The big established players did not welcome a newcomer like Grace. For one thing, she knew the business *too well!* Macquarie tried to stop her; 2GB had given her her big break, and now she was double-crossing them. In fact, twelve months would pass before 2GB broadcast its first Grace Gibson show, *Mr & Mrs North*. Artransa and EMI were ranged against her. But Grace did more than survive; she flourished.

The first four audition discs she cut were sold nationally. Ron Randell compered Grace's first show, *Here Are The Facts*. Sim Rubensohn's client Sterling Pharmaceutical bought Grace's second show, *Drama of Medicine*, and ran it nationally in both Australia and New Zealand. They showed remarkable foresight; these dramatised self-contained quarter-hour stories of heroic doctors, nurses, and significant medical discoveries continued for a total of 768 episodes over 15 years. The show was sold throughout the world and eventually in America. Another Hansen-Rubensohn client bought her third show — a series of self-contained half-hour plays bannered *Nyal Radio Playhouse*. Grace's fourth show, *Mr and Mrs North*, went to air in September 1945. Soon after, the J. Walter Thompson advertising agency bought Grace's first daytime serial, *Hollywood Holiday*, for national sponsorship by Kolynos toothpaste. Grace's company was up and flying. And every show she recorded ended with the words: "A Grace Gibson Radio Production". It was a masterstroke of publicity. Soon that phrase would resonate in the minds of the Australian radio audience.

In those early days, of course, Grace did not have enough money to build her own recording studio. Instead, she first recorded at AWA, and then hired the Australian Recording Company studio in Savoy House. The bills came in weekly, and credit terms extended for a whole seven days. Meanwhile, the advertising agencies paid her for the sponsored shows. They charged the sponsors for the production and airtime. They also paid the stations. Fortunately, the agencies mostly paid on time. Later, when Grace sold programmes direct to the stations, they were good paymasters too. Most of the stations paid on a regular day of the month. Which was good. Because, as you're about to find out, Grace was always counting the pennies between cheques.

Episode 2

Counting Pennies

DESPITE the fact I was in awe of her, Grace and I shared many things in common — especially a deep respect for money. Her tough background in El Paso had accustomed her to hardship. Likewise, my family life had been one of struggle.

HOME was Daceyville, a southern suburb of Sydney, seven kilometres from the CBD as the crow flies, not that many crows resided there. Australians, Brits, and Irish did, with household incomes well below the national weekly median. The suburb was named after John Rowland Dacey. Butcher, blacksmith, coachbuilder, Dacey was a state Labor parliamentarian who campaigned for low-cost housing for working-class people. He envisioned the creation of a garden suburb modelled on the garden city of Letchford in London. The plan came into being after his death in 1912. The suburb was opened up during the First World War. The homes were built as rental properties, and my parents were the first residents in our particular home, a semi-detached cottage. It had a good-sized lounge room, two bedrooms, and front and back verandahs. A large pantry was located on the back verandah. As the family grew, my father closed in the front verandah to make an extra bedroom. Later he covered in the rear of the house so we could store our bikes out of the rain.

The old tramline opened in 1913, with services to Circular Quay via Waterloo, with an extension to Maroubra Beach. Rosebery Racecourse was a famous local landmark, until it later became a housing estate. The Lakes Golf Course was next to the East Lakes Club, adjoining a large sand dump and a hill. Neighbouring suburbs included Kingsford, named in honour of the aviator Charles Kingsford Smith, and Pagewood, our own Hollywood where Australian movies were shot and Holden cars were made.

I was born on 8 May 1929, the youngest of five brothers. The others were Alf, Frank, Lex, and Keith. I was the youngest by four and a half years. My eldest brother was thirteen years older than me. My aunt (my father's sister) also lived in the area. Her husband was killed at Gallipoli, an original Anzac, and I was named after him — Reginald Jack.

In those days, my father — Alfred Edward James — worked in the Post Office. I think he was in charge of local telephone services. He left the Post Office around the mid 1920s to go into business with his brother, a plumber. Then came the Depression. The business suffered badly and closed down. Like so many others, Dad got work wherever he could find it. It was a tough time for a family with five children. My eldest brother had no choice but to leave school and start work when he was just thirteen.

Despite hardships, life had magic to it. Our backyard was big enough to accommodate a fowl house, a peach and fig tree, and a dog and magpie. Our crescent had a large triangle of grass in the middle, perfect for lots of games. School was only one hundred metres away down the lane. Behind the school stretched a very large paddock that led to sand hills and bush land, the East Lakes golf course, and a big lake. What more could young boys want? Every Empire Day we had cracker night, complete with a big bonfire for which we collected rubbish from the neighbours and cut down bushes from the scrubland. Milk was delivered twice a day, and bread once. In the school holidays we helped the deliverymen and got to ride with them in their horse and carts. A rabbito and an iceman also made their rounds. For a young boy like me, life was all too good to be true — with one notable exception.

My academic record was atrocious, to put it mildly. I went to Daceyville Public School, thence Randwick High for my secondary education, where I never really settled in. I was too immature, I think, and the changes of teacher for each different period confused me. And if I did not like a particular teacher, then I did not work. I also missed my old friends from Daceyville.

I did not dislike school; I *hated* it with a vengeance! Nor did it help that my handwriting was never good. I was left-handed and never corrected. I tried to write the same way as right-handed boys did, but it did not work. It was a problem especially at high school. I remember a history teacher would not give me a pass in the exam unless I wrote it all out again. On one occasion I threw an ice block at a friend who ducked. It hit my French teacher full in the face. She was not happy.

After the Intermediate Certificate — in those days, year three of high school — I left. I'm sure the principal and teachers were pleased to see my back. It is strange that I remain proud of Randwick High School. It was only the teachers who spoiled it!

I was fifteen when I found my first job. I joined a publishing company called Carlyle Stephens, where they were working on a book called *The Australian Blue Book*. It was designed as an aid for country people, and contained information about everything they would ever need. Unfortunately, the principals were not particularly honest people. Two of them were arrested for fraud when the company went broke, and I was out of a job. Our advertising manager suggested I start an advertising course.

When I was still very young, we could not afford a wireless so my first encounter with radio serials was through a neighbour's window. She used to let my friends and me listen to her radio from the garden.

Eventually we did buy a set in 1936, and the day that great big box arrived I was over the moon. To this day, I have no idea what it cost my parents. As an avid fan, I lapped up the serials, comedy shows, the *Nyal Radio Playhouse*, and the Macquarie Sunday night plays. I listened to those shows every week and got to know the names of the actors and actresses. The other show I listened to and loved was the first hit parade, Alan Toohey's *Australia's Choice*. Toohey was a great announcer with a very smooth delivery. In fact, all the announcers at 2UE seemed to me to be the best in Sydney for a long time. And later, thanks to a programme on 2GB titled *Operatic Tenors*, I developed a great love for operatic performances — not exactly what you would expect to do in Daceyville.

Small wonder I could not believe my luck to be working for Grace Gibson!

MY FATHER ended up selling life insurance. He passed away in 1959. He was five years older than Mum. She had a hard life too, raising five of her own children, as well as a niece when her sister died early. My mother was a very determined, dominant woman. She needed to be. Being the baby of the family, I spent a lot more time with her than my brothers. My brothers also served in World War II, so they were away for long periods of time. I was left behind with my parents, and I missed a lot of time with my brothers. Mum's death was a very sad time for all of us. She got sick quickly. She just seemed to fade away, and died at 73. She passed away in the family home, where I was still living at the time. She missed two important weddings. First there was mine — she died a month before I got married. Then my niece, my eldest brother's daughter, was married three or four days after Mum passed away. She was due to get married on the Saturday in the church where we wanted to have the funeral. It would have been too harrowing for everyone, so the minister, who knew us well, suggested we have the funeral at the church in Kingsford instead, the same church where I had been to Sunday school.

Our lives very much revolved around the church and all its activities. The Kingsford church was our first church, but we had left it for the one in Kensington — St Martin's Anglican Church — because my elder brothers had met some girls there so we were dragged along too. It all happened at St Martin's! Three of my brothers married two sisters and one cousin who all lived around the corner from the church. And then a fourth brother married a girl from two streets away; his wife later died of leukemia at the age of 32, and he married again just three months before I got married. Until he passed away recently, they had been married for around fifty-three years.

That church was the centre of our universe. We had a soccer team, a tennis club, a boys' gym, and were also members of the choir. We were there virtually six days a week. On Saturdays we went to the local cinema where I loved the westerns. (I still do.)

My eldest brother got married when I was ten. Not long after, two others left for the War and got married while it was still on. Keith only got married after he came back. I got to spend a lot more time with Keith, who was the next one up from me. He looked after me and did a lot to help me, and did not seem to object. He died recently. We were a very, very close family, even though we fought like cats and dogs. My two eldest brothers used to argue a lot. One picked on the other deliberately just to fuel an argument. There were quite a few rows over me apparently.

I was the only child who left the area after I got married. I moved to the North Shore, while the others had settled down in Kingsford, Kensington, and Maroubra. One of them did not approve of my new address; he told me in no uncertain terms that the North Shore was for "silvertails". Later, he himself moved to Greenwich and then St Ives!

SO THERE I was, the boy from Daceyville, duplicating Grace Gibson's scripts and putting them together into sets for the actors. It took a lot of time. I had a little hand-operated Roneo machine. It was terrible. The typists would cut stencils that I placed into the Roneo machine; as I turned the handle, ink was forced through the holes in the stencils and onto the paper. In those days I used to wear a tie. And because they got stained with ink from that wretched machine, I was always buying new ties. When the machine broke down, my hands were black and we had to send for the mechanics. So much for the glamour of radio — although I did get to meet Kitty Bluett and Ron Randell when they came in to record a *Caltex Star Theatre* play!

To save money, Grace had discovered a source for newsprint. Newsprint was not as white as ordinary paper and, as I soon discovered, was notoriously difficult to use in a duplicator. However, it was about *three* shillings a ream as against eight shillings for white paper. I had to go to the paper factory by tram and bring back six reams at a time. Actors lustily complained that it crackled when the pages were turned and, compared to white paper, it was hard to read from. But in those immediate post-War years, when money was short, Grace kept using it. To heck with the actors!

When I started, I had one wooden cabinet for storing the discs. After about three or four months, with more shows entering production, she had to buy me another cabinet. Our office space was reduced accordingly. I only did sound effects two or three times before they decided to get another boy — Doug Pickering — to do the effects and assist Reg Johnston. Doug had been at 2UE and I knew him; he was a very happy person and later left to join 2CH as a salesman. Michael Plant replaced him.

Meanwhile, Grace seemed to find different (and difficult) jobs for me to do, but I was always treated as an important member of the staff. It was quite incredible. I think I stopped printing scripts after about twelve months. By then we had a lot more programmes on air and the scheduling arrangements became more complex. I was also entrusted to deliver the cumbersome sixteen-inch transcriptions to the post office and the TAA airline counter around the corner in Phillip Street. Carrying them by hand was sometimes very heavy work. Then we started using a second airline (Ansett-ANA) that was situated about a mile from the office. No wonder Grace had chosen me over the smaller boy!

She had a shortage of money for a long time. While some people joked about Grace being mean, I knew that she had grown up when times were tough, and what she earned she protected. On the other hand, I, more than any other person, can vouch for her generosity over many, many years. Grace had that special something that drew people to her, and importantly, she loved radio drama. She was an ordinary person insofar as she knew what kind of radio ordinary people liked, and she could look at a script and see its values, and if she said it was not good, it was not. She was the only person who went about sales as though nothing else mattered. She attracted important people like Frank Packer. She belonged in the smart set, and men were attracted to her charms. She had this dynamic personality, but she was not good looking. She was handsome, which better describes her than attractive. I never believed she relied on her sex to gain any advantage in business, and she was very loyal to the man she married; she adored him for the rest of her life.

NOT only did Grace watch every penny, she expected her staff to do the same. In those days before the advent of tape recording, radio shows were cut straight onto disc. A mistake meant going back and starting again with a fresh disc. The first time I did sound effects, I came down from the ARC studio and Grace laughingly asked me if I had caused any recuts. I said that on that episode we had three; I caused two, and one of the actors the other. She did not look too pleased.

My salary was not a lot of money but it got me through. I was able to pay my mother something and keep something for myself — not much, but it was enough. I think in those days we did not worry terribly much about money, so long as we had enough to do what we wanted to do, get us to places, see a movie, and so on. We did not care much; we did not save much either. It was just a nice living.

Grace never paid overtime to her staff; she paid overtime only to actors if Actors Equity regulations called for it. But for the rest of us, she just wanted us to do what had to be done and that was all there was to it. Yes, she was manipulative, but that was Grace. All part of the package. For example, some of my duties were bizarre. In winter I had to fill the kerosene heaters in the office. When the office closed for Christmas, I was expected to man the phones in case any overseas orders came in; while I was there, I repainted the office. When Grace held a charity function, I was barman and waiter. It was also my job to go to the ice works late on Friday afternoon with a taxi truck, fill it with ice, and deliver it to the venue. And every Christmas, when Grace sent a bottle of whisky to each of the Sydney radio and advertising agency executives with whom she did business, it was my task to make the deliveries. Can you guess the name of the whisky? What else — but a bottle of Old Parr!

Every year, Grace treated the staff to a Christmas lunch at the American Club, where Grace was a foundation member. It was a company tradition and sparked new stories about Grace's tightfistedness. Scriptwriter Ross Napier and I always had a couple of beers beforehand, because she was so mean with the liquor. If we ordered a second drink she would say, "But you've had one already." Ross called her "the most ungracious hostess". Then again, she was just being Grace.

Sometimes Grace's penny-pinching was almost laughable. She went through every item on my expense account with a ruler. Once she demanded all my tram tickets to and from 2UW as proof of petty cash claims. I very politely reminded her that had I wanted to cheat, I could have *walked* to 2UW and picked up discarded tickets off the street. It was one of the only times I saw Grace speechless.

She was fiercely loyal to her staff. One of the boys from ARC used to occasionally come downstairs to listen to different episodes of our shows in his lunch hour. I did not mind, and always let him in. On one particular day he called in and I said, "Sorry, I cannot play any shows today because I have got a visitor." Scriptwriter Ross Napier was there. The ARC boy objected so strongly that in the end I threw him out. On another occasion I was upstairs at ARC waiting for a couple of urgent transcriptions and a couple of the lads deliberately held things up. I got mad and stormed out saying something like, "Typical of AR bloody C!" George Aiken, ARC's general manager, was in the corridor and heard my outburst. The next thing you know he was downstairs complaining to Grace about what I had said. Grace's answer was, "Well, if Reg said it, it *must* be true …"

On reflection, I did have a special relationship with Grace, and it started very early, but it certainly had its authoritarian moments. For example, she made me buy a bottle of milk for morning tea. I was not allowed to have a tea or coffee with the girls. I had to have milk! Maybe she thought I need calcium to strengthen my bones, so I could keep carrying all those heavy transcriptions.

Another time at a Christmas lunch I was having a cigarette. She told me to put it out and demanded that I hand over the rest of the pack. She said I was not to smoke anymore, while she sat at the table and finished off all my cigarettes. And to the best of my knowledge, Grace was *not* a smoker!

GRACE handled all the major sales in those early days. When audition discs were made, she set out to interest sponsors or networks to buy them nationally, or she would sell the shows directly to capital city stations. We had agents in Melbourne and Brisbane who did local sales there, but it was all really left to her. The agents just handled the accounts and not really too much else.

Oddly enough — and this will indicate just how much trust Grace placed on my young shoulders — she left it to me to choose which episodes to use for audition purposes. Obviously she would always try to play prospective clients the first two episodes of any new show, but it was not always possible. Because we ordered only six pressings of each episode, those first episodes might have been out doing the rounds of station playing schedules; the discs might not come back to the office for six months, if at all. So my job became the selection of subsequent episodes to play prospective clients. I was quite proud of this. Grace never once queried my selections. After all, I had read the scripts while I was Roneo-ing and sorting them, and I had listened to all the new pressings when they came down from ARC. I probably knew more about the different series than anybody else. Grace gave me responsibilities like these very early in the piece. Even when we needed a new duplicating machine, Grace entrusted me to buy it. Whatever I needed she gave to me, as long as I could give her sensible reasons why. That is how it went along. Eventually we outgrew cabinets for storing discs; I controlled the despatch department, which became immense over the years. I had two boys working for me. From that one shared office we ultimately grew into three other offices — *just* for the despatch department!

But let us be clear: Grace was nobody's fool. She was very attractive to men, especially powerful men. They loved her. I never thought she was that attractive, but she had a presence without being conventionally good-looking. Her accent could put you off too. Obviously, she had a certain magic about her.

After her break from Artransa, there had been a fair amount of ill feeling about her but I never saw any of that. 2GB still bought our programmes, and she continued getting on well with managing director Stan Clark. Let's put it this way – if it was a man, she got on very well with him. When she was still living at Elizabeth Bay, she never went home early on Thursdays. She used to let a particular radio station executive go there for the afternoon for a private tryst with one of her lady friends. He was having a nice affair with her at Grace's apartment!

COUNTING the pennies, Grace ordered no more than six transcription discs for each episode. (After all, each disc cost 16/- to press.) Surprisingly, our discs were generally returned in good condition; discs were only destroyed as a last resort. Some shows like *Dossier on Dumetrius* sold so well that even Grace finally conceded that six discs were inadequate. Meanwhile, New Zealand needed six pressings of everything; they had to schedule broadcasts over about 30 stations.

Of course, *Dr Paul* broke all the rules; it was nationally sponsored on 40 stations. And because all the stations played the same episode on the same day right around Australia, *40* copies were pressed of every episode. When the stations returned the discs after broadcast, my despatch department bulged at the seams.

ON AVERAGE, each quarter-hour episode cost £25 to produce — including the script, the cast, cutting a master, and pressing transcription discs.

In order to earn back their production cost, Grace's shows had to sell in Sydney, Melbourne, and Brisbane. A New Zealand sale ensured a profit. That was our rule of thumb; Grace got her money back on the Australian sales, but made her profits on the overseas ones.

Each station licensed the disc from us for *one* on-air broadcast, after which the station was contractually bound to send the disc to the next station on the schedule. That is why broadcasts were always scheduled with a fortnight's "safety buffer" between stations. Each station had a copy of the schedule and knew where each disc was coming from, and where it had to go next. And each station footed the bill for freight. If a country station finished playing a disc on Thursday morning, it had to be packed and wrapped by Friday latest and sent to the next station. If there was a direct train line from one town to another, we tried to schedule broadcasts accordingly so the stations could easily send the discs to the next station. At any given moment, there were hundreds of discs circulating around Australia by airfreight, rail, and parcel post. Fortunately, very few discs ever ran late or got lost.

If a national sponsor were involved, the sponsor paid the freight charges. We charged the sponsor for sending the disc to the first station on the schedule, and then each station in turn billed the sponsor as the disc made its way around the network. Often, the sponsor's agency such as Lintas or J. Walter Thompson despatched and circulated the discs themselves. Discs had to be shipped back at the stations' cost.

However, the Major Network — 2UE Sydney, 3DB Melbourne, and their affiliates — was a different matter. It bought the broadcast rights nationally for five years, but it also had the rights to *on-sell* the show. In other words, if Major paid £30 an episode, all they were interested in was recouping their £30. They would sell episodes for as little as 4/- each and we could not do anything about it. After five years we would get the rights back, and then it would be a whole new ball game. When I became sales manager later on, these were the complications I had to deal with!

BY THE way, to save Grace even more pennies, I recycled all the corrugated cardboard packaging that came back from stations and the Australian Record Company. I taped the Gibson label over the other labels. We charged the stations two shillings for packing as well as freight costs. Call it my Daceyville training; I hated to waste money or spend it unnecessarily. Years later, when Grace sold the company, the new owner's accountant rang me. "This is ridiculous," he said. I asked him, "What's ridiculous?" And he told me, "I was going through all your figures, and you're making a profit out of packing." Well, *old habits die hard!*

Counting all those pennies became increasingly complex. I had started out working from my table in the main office, controlling the orderly circulation of hundreds of transcription discs around Australia. By the end of the 1940s, my title was Despatch Manager and I had two offices full of transcriptions as well as an assistant. By the time Grace moved the company to Hunter Street, her staff numbered seventeen and I had a library of 30,000 discs stored in three rooms back in Savoy House, from where we despatched them. That was not the only change. In the 1950s, our new shows were released on LP (long-play) records with outside starts, but the old 16-inch discs with inside starts were still being used; they were stored in a rented garage in Kensington. At first we had one quarter-hour episode per side on 10-inch LPs. Then we moved to 12-inch LPs, with two quarter-hour episodes per side, or a complete half-hour episode per side.

NO MATTER how adept I became at counting pennies, accidents did happen. For example, The Case of the Guiding Light!

Grace was launching a new serial — *The Guiding Light* — and decided to send out a photograph of an ornate lamp with the audition discs and publicity material. She borrowed the lamp from a friend, Madame Du Boulay, who ran an antiques shop in Sydney. Once it was photographed, Grace decided that the only person who could be trusted to return the lamp safely was dependable Reg James. (You can see where this is heading, I'm sure!) So we packed the lamp and away I went. As I stepped out of the lift in our building, a speeding man crashed into me. I was quite sure the impact had broken the lamp. Sick to the stomach, I kept going to Madame Du Boulay's shop and blurted out what I thought had happened. We unwrapped the parcel and sure enough there was her lamp — in a hundred pieces. I mumbled a million apologies, beat a hasty retreat, and fronted up to Grace. When she heard my story, she was not cranky — *shocked* would be a better word. She was obviously thinking, "This couldn't happen!" I was traumatised; I left her office, ready to resign, and ducked into the nearest pub. When I got home that evening, Grace was on the line. She said I should not worry about the lamp. Then I got a call from Madame Du Boulay to say the lamp had not been worth that much anyway so "don't give it a thought". Fortunately, the Madame had not tried to inflate the lamp's value and demand compensation from Grace. If she had, I think I would have resigned on the spot!

RADIO production soared to dizzying heights in the 1950s. Everything had to be recorded in Australia. Imported shows would not be allowed on air again until later. Now her cash flow problems had eased, but Grace never once stopped counting the pennies. And frankly, neither did I. Just as well. One never knew what vicissitudes lay ahead.

Episode 3

The Reg Johnston Years

REG JOHNSTON set the standard for Grace Gibson. He crafted every show meticulously, from rigorous script approval, choosing exactly the right voices, finding the most emotive, appropriate music, even down to the nuances of sound effects. He never skimped on the tiniest detail; "that'll do" was not in his DNA. Reg invested each show with a unique aural atmosphere that you could cut with a knife — like the dramatic tom-tom beats for *Night Beat*, the overall *noir* sound, and the integration of superlative acting with music. He and Grace were on the same page, two steely, demanding minds in search of perfection. I carried Reg Johnston's standard in my mind for the rest of my career. I became the keeper of the flame. I would listen to a show and ask, *Is this what Reg Johnston would have done?*

REG WAS more than Grace's first production manager — he was the artistic soul of the company. His radio career began when he walked in off the street to ask about a job at 2GB, and was hired on the spot. From cadet announcer he was soon scriptwriting, producing and compering Macquarie Network shows. His talent was in constant demand. Advertising agency J. Walter Thompson hired him to do all the commercial announcing for Lux and the *Amateur Hour*. Next came a year at 2UE as assistant producer to Paul Jacklin, the programme manager, after which he freelanced as a writer, narrator and producer for the ABC.

When Grace hired Johnston to direct *Hollywood Holiday* and adapt American scripts for *Mr & Mrs North,* one of radio's greatest partnerships began. Australian actor Alan White summed up their working relationship perfectly: "Reg and Grace were peas in a pod in their tastes and enthusiasm. They were both workaholics. I can never remember them disagreeing."

Grace so relied on Reg that she was constantly frightened that something bad might happen to him. She always fretted about his ferry trip to and from work, upbraiding him for his habit of taking a briefcase stuffed with scripts home to Mosman every night. "What if the ferry sinks, or you drop the scripts overboard?" She had good reason to be fearful. Thanks to Reg, her shows dominated the ratings, starting in 1946 with Reg Johnston's production of *The Shadow.* A malevolent chuckling voice, accompanied by a Phantom-of-the-Opera organ, introduced each half-hour episode with the words: "Who knows what evil lurks in the hearts of men? *The Shadow* knows!" Lloyd Lamble acted the title role.

By 1947 Reg was directing *Nyal Radio Playhouse, Out of the Night, The Shadow, Caltex Star Theatre, Till the End of Time, Tales of the Supernatural,* and *Drama of Medicine.* And the standards he set were admired across the industry.

Reg respected the actors' talent and they in turn respected him. Michael Pate believed Reg Johnston had "a nice fluidness" to his direction. John Woodward, the senior panel operator at the Australian Record Company, said Reg's challenges were endless; "He pretty well drove me up the wall with his search for perfection, but he achieved it." Peter Yeldham — one of Australia's best scriptwriters and now a great Australian novelist — was definitely more in awe of Reg Johnston than he was of Grace Gibson; "It was Reg who would say yes, we want to use you, or no, we don't. I don't remember how many scripts I wrote when

Reg was there, but I was always nervous about how they were going to be received."

Unfortunately for the casting girl, Reg was uncompromising. If he told her the actors he wanted for the three leading characters of a half-hour play and they were not available, he would say, "Go to buggery, I won't do it, get another script." Bearing in mind that a lot of actors did not have telephones in those early days, the casting girl's job was made even harder.

THE LAST thing I expected as the office junior was for Reg Johnston to ask my opinion. When he made a new show, I remember him calling me in to listen to the voice auditions. Even me, at 16 or 17, he wanted *my* opinion, and it was damn hard to give someone like that your opinion of the acting ability of Alan White or Michael Pate. When I started with the company, Reg Johnston was paid £25 a week. It was very good money. I used to bank £5 a week for him.

Fortunately, Reg made all his script corrections in pencil. I remember the day when a writer friend wanted a rejected script returned. Reg — in panic — gave me the script with hurried instructions to clean it up. Just as well I had a good eraser, because the script was covered in annotations!

Radio *was* Reg Johnston's life. He was young, enthusiastic, and the word "compromise" was not in his vocabulary. I might be prejudiced, but when I started at Grace Gibson's we were all in one office. Reg was just about to commence production of a new show, *The Story of Flight*, sponsored by Qantas. I was just a few feet away from Reg so I heard everything that went on. I was not intentionally eavesdropping; I had to hear it because I was there. People like Kath Carroll would come in, and they would have a discussion about her ideas, what she was writing for next week. And Alan White would come in and discuss his roles with Reg, and they would go through them. Reg directed the early book adaptations too. Every day I was treated to a master class on radio production.

DOSSIER ON DUMETRIUS was Grace's greatest triumph — thanks to Reg Johnston's foresight. Melbourne-based scriptwriter Lindsay Hardy had offered the concept to his good friend, producer Donovan Joyce. For some reason, Don passed on it. When Lindsay offered it to us, Reg Johnston saw its potential instantly. How right he was. Even today people still associate Grace's name with that show more than any other. It began production in 1950, and was first broadcast over 2UE on 5 February 1951. It played on 2UE two or three times, on 2UW about four or five times, and on 2GB, and at least five times in Melbourne, four times in Brisbane, and every country station in Australia would have played it once, sometimes twice. In fact, I cannot recall one Australian radio station outside of the capital cities that did not play this show at least once. It was so popular, and so engrossing, that often country cinemas would not start their evening screening until that day's broadcast of *Dossier* had concluded.

At the time Reg began production, World War II had only been over for half a dozen years, and the Cold War was the new reality. *Dossier on Dumetrius*, the first of five shows featuring the character Major Gregory George Athelstone Keen of MI5, was set in post-World War II London and ran for 104 quarter-hour episodes. Keen is searching for a million dollars' worth of Nazi loot. Also in the hunt are master criminal Dumetrius and his personal assassin Yottie Blum, together with his beautiful mistress Hedy Bergner.

Apparently Lindsay got the idea for Gregory Keen after meeting a secret service agent in England at the end of World War II. To my thinking, Keen was as exciting a character as James Bond, whom he pre-dated. *Dossier on Dumetrius* was followed by *Deadly Nightshade*, set in Sydney in the 1950s with Keen assigned to search for a missing scientist who disappeared in the Outback. Later, *Twenty-Six Hours* captured the tension of Cold War Berlin. The action takes place over a night and a day, and the fall of another night. The diaries of a warmongering American general provide the background, and Lindsay made it quite obvious he did not like Americans!

Reg Johnston cast Bruce Stewart as Keen, Dinah Shearing as Hedy, Frank Waters as Coutts, and Guy Doleman as Dumetrius. Bruce played Keen in the first shows; Allan Trevor took over in the last two. Guy Doleman was a drinking buddy of Lindsay Hardy and Don Joyce, and was Lindsay's favourite actor. He had risen to fame in Australian movies and radio serials such as *Hagen's Circus*; like so many other Australian actors of the era, he went overseas and flourished. Guy's best-known role was as Count Lippe in the 1965 James Bond film *Thunderball*. He then played Colonel Ross in three movie adaptations of Len Deighton's Harry Palmer novels starring Michael Caine. When you look at Guy's acting credits — *The Ipcress File*, *Funeral in Berlin*, and *Enigma*, to name a few — you can appreciate Reg Johnston's eye for quality acting.

After a stint overseas, Lindsay Hardy returned to Australia in the late 1950s. This time, Don Joyce was not going to let him slip through his fingers again. Lindsay wrote two new Gregory Keen serials for him: *Two Roads to Samarra*, which had a Scottish backdrop, while *Smell of Terror* was set in the Caribbean. We acted as distributor on those shows.

ALAN White, Michael Pate, and Dinah Shearing were the stars of a stage play that Reg directed at the Mosman Town Hall. It was called *Amphitryon 38*, by the French dramatist Jean Giraudoux. The play is about the god Jupiter intruding into the faithful marriage of two mortals. (Hardly *Dr Paul* material!) It was a great show, and ended with Alan tearing Dinah's gown as the curtain came down.

On the final night, however, the curtain was late in coming down. When Alan tore Dinah's gown she was left on stage half-naked. I am quite sure the curtain was late deliberately — after all, it was the last night, and Alan had a wicked gleam in his eye!

WITHOUT warning, Reg Johnston got very sick. He had directed the first twelve episodes of *Night Beat* and twenty episodes of *Dossier on Dumetrius*. He had also directed the audition episodes of *Dr Paul* and *Portia Faces Life*. Suddenly everything stopped.

Grace obtained the services of veteran producer Lawrence H. Cecil, who had been freelancing at 2GB. His credits at Macquarie were impressive. Lawrie Cecil stepped in and took over the reins. The problem was that Lawrie had such a good name. Very soon I, for one, realised that his best years were behind him. *Long behind him!* He used to come in in the morning and direct *Night Beat*, then go to the Imperial Services Club for lunch, and you never saw him again. He kept his casts in line firmly, some might say brutally. And he was utterly useless as our production manager. Alan White said to me one time after recording a *Night Beat* episode that Lawrie could not give him anything. "I didn't get anything in the way of direction when I did a show for him." Alan was a very serious, collaborative actor, and he respected the work more than the director did! I hate to say it, but I wish we had never let Lawrence H. Cecil in.

REG'S SUDDEN death from kidney failure in 1951 was a devastating blow. He was only 32 years old.

To my mind, he was before his time. He wanted to do semi-documentaries, true stuff, educational *as well as* entertaining. Grace was blessed to have had him. He nurtured actors like Alan White, Michael Pate, and John Bushelle. They were the young people, radio was their life, and they were really living it, and they wanted to go somewhere with it. Alan White perfectly summed up the Reg Johnston-Grace Gibson partnership in a letter he wrote to me from London in December

2003: "Above professionalism rises a rare form of genius. I've seen it [in Britain] with (Sir) Richard Eyre, (Sir) Trevor Nunn, and (Sir) Peter Hall, and both Grace and Reg had it, and were as unaware of it as the others were. The big beneficiaries of this are the audiences, who will always remember the shows they produced."

Reg Johnston was a perfectionist *and* a professional. In the afternoon before the next day's recording he went upstairs to the Australian Record Company studio, auditioned the music with the panel operator, and checked out the sound effects. On the morning of the recording, he took his time but got precisely what he wanted. Later, Michael Plant applied the same discipline. But after Reg died, we lost that dedication. It certainly never happened with Lawrie Cecil. It happened with John Saul to a certain extent, but he got himself sidetracked with Method acting, and he actually stuffed up quite a few shows with it.

Looking back, I think the directors were the big weakness of Australian radio drama. If you got a great show it was more likely because of the panel operator. I think the panel operators were the true heroes of radio drama. At ARC, it would take just two hours to rehearse, record and finish a half-hour episode of *Night Beat*. In my experience, panel operators (often self-trained) did all the preparation work, selecting the music and sound effects; then during the recording they timed the episode, cued the artists, set the levels, and operated up to seven turntables. They could not make mistakes because they cost money and wasted time; any technical mistakes were the responsibility of the recording company. In many respects, these panel operators were virtually the director. When our panel operator Peter Benardos was at Macquarie, he received an on-air credit for his work on the Macquarie play *The Sound Barrier*. Peter had operated eight turntables simultaneously — live to air, without a mistake — creating the effects of speeding jet aircraft. I believe it was the only time that a panel operator was given such recognition. When we had two panel operators on staff, one would be recording programmes in the morning while the other was preparing to record in the afternoon. Then the one who had been in the studio all morning would do the preparation for the next morning's recordings. It was meticulous and highly creative work, and it was crucial to the final sound and emotional impact of a show.

The truth is, the panel operators were so good that the directors just sat there, along for the ride. Some of the people who directed were not really sincere.

Episode 4

The Big Shows

RADIO drama was the theatre of the mind. And to every listener, it offered a different personal experience. In a radio drama, the writer's first task was to paint a picture of the characters that each of us will "see" differently. As an insider, when I hear a show like *Dossier on Dumetrius*, I can picture the actors because I knew them personally. But for a general radio audience, each listener would create his or her own mental image of each character. And that is the crux of good radio drama; making each listener feel as if he or she is being spoken to as an individual. And, just as different sounds evoke different images, different voices and accents also evoke different images. The manner in which a word is spoken can vary so much — more than a word in a manuscript that is simply underlined, italicized, or set in bold.

Characterisation was the most important ingredient. The characters are the glue that holds everything together. A hero did not have to be good; he could have faults, and he could have affairs, which were usually the fault of women. The most necessary character was a bitch, someone that women could hate! Good wholesome women did not make a popular radio character — there is nothing less interesting to a predominantly female audience than a happy, well-adjusted woman. Great radio characters have to appeal very strongly to the listener's emotions.

In the best serials, a number of storylines involving a variety of characters will be running simultaneously at any given time. The way these myriad pathways integrate is how a narrative is created. A powerful narrative combined with believable characters can make a vivid impact, especially when the creator has a strong desire to convince the audience of themes and social issues.

As part of the writing discipline, character names had to be used in dialogue constantly to eliminate any confusion about who was speaking to whom, especially for those tuning in midway through an episode. And every episode *had* to finish on a cliffhanger. It might sound unbelievable, but a lot of writers could not do that. A lot of writers could not write for Grace Gibson.

Sound effects were used to convey happenings. More than that, they helped paint the picture and construct an atmosphere. Some effects were taken from library discs; others were created in the studio at the time of recording. Take the sound of someone walking on gravel; the footsteps could be stealthy, or running to escape danger — this was the art of the sound effects man.

Narrations helped the mind concentrate and visualise the scene being described. The narrator's main job, however, was to remind listeners of what had happened previously. Ron Roberts was, to my mind, the epitome of a great narrator.

The opening track of a serial, sometimes as short as 30 seconds, signalled to listeners that one of their favourite shows was about to begin. It was followed by a commercial, and then the main story would continue. Grace Gibson always ensured that the opening tracks of her programmes attracted immediate attention — the best examples being the tom-tom beats introducing another episode of *Night Beat*, and the sound of cattle being herded along with whip cracks that opened every episode of *Cattleman*. Directors spent a lot of time on the theme music, the voice of the narrator, and of course the words themselves.

Decades after some of these tracks were last heard on air, people can still remember them. Listeners of a certain generation will always tell you, "Only *The Shadow* knows …"

HAVING heard virtually every episode of every show we ever made, it is quite easy for me to nominate our best programmes — but not in any particular order:

Dossier on Dumetrius
Cattleman
The Castlereagh Line
Night Beat
Dragnet
For the Defence
Medical File
The Bishop's Mantle
Till the End of Time
Tales of the Supernatural

Perhaps I should not say this, but I was never terribly keen on the long-running serials like *Dr Paul*. Naturally, though, these were not aimed at people like me anyway. But they were massively successful. Grace Gibson was the major name in daytime serials. The two longest-running commercial serials were *Dr Paul* (4,634 episodes) and *Portia Faces Life* (3,544 episodes). In *Dr Paul's* case, that represented over 22 years of continuous broadcast.

I did not have a particular genre that was my favourite; anything with a good story and quality acting won me. In fact, the acting influenced me a lot. Book adaptations were one of Grace's signatures. One of my favourites was *The Bishop's Mantle* with Michael Pate. Others included *Frenchman's Creek* and *Dinner at Antoine's*. I always found the self-contained 15-minute shows appealing too, such as *Tales of the Supernatural*, *Australian Stories*, and *Tales of the Campfire*.

FROM the 1930s to the early 1950s, daytime serials were played four days a week, Monday to Thursday. Why not Fridays? In those days, most women were out shopping — which often meant a big day with a trip to the city where all the major department stores were located. On Fridays, stations offered a general programme including community singing. By the mid 1950s, when bigger suburban shopping centres were springing up everywhere, drama was on the air *five* days a week. The old Friday trip to the city was a thing of the past.

Traditionally, we recorded episodes 1 and 2 of any new programme once Grace had given the scripts her blessing. As soon as a sponsor or network purchased it, and once an on-air commencement date was determined, a broadcast schedule was worked out and adhered to by the production team. Each programme was allocated a different morning or afternoon of the week for recording. We would record four or five quarter-hours of one show in the morning, then the same for another programme in the afternoon. For example, *Dr Paul* was always recorded on Thursday mornings. We kept strictly to those schedules because the actors' agents needed to know what their time commitment would be. We worked on being six weeks ahead of broadcast. The six weeks were to allow us to be far enough ahead in production to keep the stations in episodes.

Christmas brought more pressure. In the early days, all the actors took three weeks off at Christmas. That meant we had to get a *further* three weeks ahead. About October we would start scheduling extra episodes into each recording session. By the week before Christmas we stopped recording, and we had sufficient discs in stock to keep the stations going over the break. Which also meant that the actors did not lose any work.

LIKE all the other local production companies, we needed overseas sales to make a decent profit. We were very careful not to set programmes — particularly daytime serials — in Australia with Australian accents. No way could *Dr Paul* speak with an Ocker accent! We used what we called the mid-Atlantic accent and the settings were what we called "Nowheresville". The cultural cringe was alive and well on radio; British and American accents and settings were acceptable, while ours were not. In fact, when we tried to change settings and accents from American to Australian in *The Shadow* and *Night Beat*, the switch was not successful and we immediately changed them back again.

The first private detective show to succeed with a local setting was Ron Beck's *I Hate Crime*, starring Ken Wayne as Larry Kent, and written by an American, Don Haring. Larry Kent was an American ex-serviceman living in Sydney. The show introduced sexual innuendo into radio. There is no doubt an Australian accent was a hindrance back in the 1940s and 50s, and I guess in those days our cities — and even the Great Barrier Reef and Kakadu — were unknown overseas.

Thinking back, *Dad and Dave* and *Search for the Golden Boomerang* were exceptions. However, in terms of contemporary cultural values, *Dad and Dave* had no indigenous characters whatsoever, while *Search for the Golden Boomerang* would not be acceptable today because of the way the Arunta people were depicted. Eventually Australian-set shows with local accents were acceptable worldwide — witness *Cattleman* and *The Castlereagh Line*, two of our best shows.

WHEN Grace had an audition disc she was happy with, it was played to Lintas, the "house" advertising agency of the mighty Lever Bros. Like other sponsors, they seemed quite happy with what we produced. They never made any suggestions or told us what to do. We simply presented them with episodes 1 and 2, and a short synopsis, and they made their decisions based on what they heard and read. Lintas snapped up the national Australian rights to *Dr Paul* for Pepsodent toothpaste. Gibson's supplied the transcription discs of each episode, which the agency distributed. The client paid for any extra discs. After playing, the discs had to be returned to Gibson's. We then kept six discs for sale to other markets. *Dr Paul* began its epic run in 1948, four mornings a week on a 40-station network selected by Lintas to deliver the maximum number of housewives around Australia. The next contract saw Lintas buy both the national Australian and New Zealand rights. Then Lintas South Africa bought the programme, starting back at episode 1. Lintas also bought the show for Fiji. The good doctor delivered even more sales. British-based broadcaster Overseas Rediffusion bought the show for Jamaica, Trinidad, Barbados, and British Guyana on behalf of Ovaltine. Singapore signed on as well, so *Dr Paul* could help the locals improve their English.

GRACE was an entrepreneur. She gathered a loyal staff around her; some of them would still be employees when she retired in 1978. She had her opinions and shaped her productions with infinite care. She focused on the scripts first. The script was God.

None of our greatest, most memorable shows could have existed without great scripts. Grace hired the best writers in the business: in the early days, Lynn Foster, Rex Rienits, Max Afford, Peter Taylor, Michael Noonan, and Phillip Mann; in the later years, Lindsay Hardy, Ross Napier, Peter Yeldham, Kathleen Carroll, Coral Lansbury, and Michael Plant. Grace admitted to me once, "I'm a crank on scripts. There's one thing I can say about myself, I can always read a script and tell whether it's any good or not for radio."

Grace had to approve the first and second episodes of every new programme, and then the writer was commissioned to go ahead with the first ten scripts, and then stop until we had sold the show. Once a show was in production, she would spot check the scripts every now and then; woe betide any writer who let the standard slip. She also took scripts home to read in bed. If she fell asleep while reading a particular script, the writer was doomed. Asked years later to nominate her best-written shows, she had no hesitation: "*Dossier on Dumetrius* and *Cattleman*. And the scripts were very, very good for *Twenty-Six Hours* and *Thirty Days Hath September*."

From my observations, Grace had an uncanny ability to put herself in the listener's place. She knew what they wanted to hear. Her long-run serials started with American scripts: *Dr Paul, Portia Faces Life, Life Can be Beautiful, The Life of Mary Sothern, The Man I Married, Girl from Nowhere,* and *Aunt Mary*. So did *Night Beat* and *Dragnet*. Self-contained programmes like the *Amazing Mr Malone, Danger Is My Business*, and *Squad Room* used American scripts exclusively. Eventually, I'm proud to say, Australian writers wrote everything.

Because radio was a new medium, writers had to learn the trade like everyone else. Back in the 1940s, star writers like Rex Rienits and Max Afford commanded £5 per script. (Max was almost before my time; an excellent writer, he scripted *Tales of the Supernatural* for Grace, the iconic *Hagen's Circus*, and a lot of work for the ABC.) Lesser names were paid £4, and some only £3. Still, it was good money. Like acting, writing was a volume business. A writer handing in 10 episodes a week at £4 each was earning an enviable income for those days.

Each quarter-hour episode had to run 12-and-a-half minutes, or 12 minutes 40 seconds maximum, leaving the balance of time for sponsors' messages. As a rule of thumb, each foolscap page of double-spaced dialogue ran one-and-a half minutes. One episode required at least eight pages. As you can imagine, the longer the serial, the harder it got. Writing a long-running serial was a monumental task requiring discipline and dedication. It was a tremendous commitment for a writer to make, one that might take years to finish, and not one that could be entered into lightly. Even in the 1950s, most Australian writers were inexperienced at this type of writing. Kathleen Carroll, Coral Lansbury, and Ross Napier were the exceptions.

KATHLEEN Carroll was a staff writer from the early days, and kept writing for Grace until the late 1960s. She worked from home because Grace did not have room for her in the office. She was a friendly, very reliable writer who quietly soldiered on in the background, turning out scripts for Grace's soapies. Her best writing for Grace were her book adaptations in association with director Reg Johnston: E. V. Timms' *Pathway of the Sun*, Frances Parkinson Keyes' *Dinner at Antoine's*, Daphne du Maurier's *Frenchman's Creek*, and Margaret Kennedy's lighthearted romance *Escape Me Never*, which starred Michael Pate and Alan White. I believe those shows were the highlight of Kath's career; I do not think she ever forgot her good association with Reg Johnston. Kath was not only a great writer of book adaptations but also long-run serials. She was also responsible for two series of court dramas. When one of her scripts failed Grace's "sleep test", Kath was very worried. Grace said, "I didn't get to the end because I fell asleep in bed. But don't worry, that always happens — if I read a good script I fall asleep." Kath always thought that was a wonderful story, but I do not think it was true!

Because I respected Kath, I called her Miss Carroll for a long time. She was a lot older than me, and had been brought up in the same way. She and her husband Harry were very left-wing Labor voters. They lived in a Paddington terrace. I had my first taste of Scotch at Kath's place. Betty Barnard and her husband (Alan Nash the trumpeter) were also there. It was after a function with Grace, and it nearly made sick. In fact, it made me *so* sick I did not try it again for years. When I did, Grace abused me after every party for drinking it and encouraged everybody else to do the same. (I was always barman and Grace would always count the empty bottles!) It is sad to think that Kath never enjoyed the "star" quality that other scriptwriters did, but for thirty years she was a major contributor to the company's success.

LIBERAL Prime Minister Malcolm Turnbull's mother Coral Lansbury was one of Sydney's most prolific serial writers. The daughter of Macquarie's sound effects guru Oscar Lansbury, Coral suddenly shocked everyone by marrying the elderly George Edwards. Later, as his vivacious young widow, she married again briefly, giving birth to Malcolm Turnbull.

One of my favourite radio yarns concerns Coral. When she decided to move to New Zealand in pursuit of an academic career and her third husband, she handed over *Portia Faces Life* to Ross Napier. She had been briefed to give Napier a synopsis of the past 100 episodes and an outline of all the characters in the story. She had done that very well — except for one minor detail: Portia Manning had a daughter. In one episode of *Portia*, Coral sent the little girl upstairs, but forgot to tell Ross. And to this day she's still up there because Ross never brought her down!

MICHAEL Plant served his apprenticeship with Grace, both as a staff writer and director. He was a brilliant young writer who — like Reg Johnston — would die in his thirties. He was on Grace's payroll briefly in the early days, as Reg Johnston's assistant, writing, doing sound effects, and directing. He was so talented that he had written, produced, and directed a one-hour version of Daphne du Maurier's *Jamaica Inn* for radio while he was still at school! Before long, he was off to England but returned some years later to write and direct more shows. (Michael's replacement was Ross Napier, who would write some of Grace's most successful programmes over the next four decades.) Grace recalled, "Michael was one of the best writers we ever had."

When Michael went to America, he wrote for the top television shows of the day such as *Bourbon Street Beat*. Returning to Australia, he created *Whiplash* and *The Mavis Bramston Show* for Channel 7. Michael's death, at the height of *The Mavis Bramston Show*, came as a bombshell. He died of an overdose of sleeping pills. Many believed he had committed suicide; I believed it was an accident.

PETER Yeldham started writing for radio at 17 when he was a messenger boy at 2GB. He used to write scripts at night, passionate to break into the industry. As Peter told me, "There was a tremendous amount of production going on. Radio was almost our only local form of entertainment. We thought in those days we were making the best radio shows in the world, and I sometimes think we were."

After writing scripts for AWA, Peter met Grace in 1950. The work soon began to mount up. *Night Beat, Drama of Medicine, Medical File*. Next, Peter conceived *For the Defence*, dramatised stories about famous defence counsels. By 1953 he was doing more work for Grace than anyone else, and writing a lot for Hilda Scurr at EMI. I remember Peter saying how Grace frequently warned him that he would price himself out of the market. He said, "When she had to pay me £25 a week, she paid through gritted teeth."

As well as Grace's shows, Peter wrote *Address Unknown*. He moved to Britain, wrote for top television dramas there, before returning to write major television shows for Hector Crawford and then turned to writing novels. He is now in his 80s, and has achieved great success. He told me that some time ago he thought about writing for radio again, but decided he could no longer do it. Well, Peter, if you change your mind, I know that some of your books would make fabulous radio serials!

LINDSAY Hardy was a superlative scriptwriter — despite his atrocious work ethic! I had to stand outside his office, with instructions not to let him out until he had finished writing. But make no mistake — despite his unpredictability, his standard *never* dropped. Lindsay's Cold War thrillers were some of Grace's most enduring shows. Centred on the character of Major Gregory Keene, Lindsay wrote five of them. *Dossier on Dumetrius* was the first; in my opinion, the last, *The Smell of Terror*, was not as good as the others. Lindsay's passion was outstanding, his scripts crisp and intelligent. Lindsay loved and believed in the characters he created, but was very fussy about the artists who portrayed them. His favourite actor was his drinking buddy Guy Doleman, and he wanted him as the villain in every show. But when Margo Lee was cast in an important role in *Deadly Nightshade*, he soon had her character strangled and out of the show. When Lindsay grew weary of his hero, he wanted to kill off Gregory Keen at the end of *Deadly Nightshade*. Grace would not hear of it. She sent him back to his typewriter for *Twenty-Six Hours*, so Lindsay contrived to have Keen shot with a dumdum shell; his hero lost his arm, in lieu of his life. (Ironically, Lindsay's own left arm had been permanently injured by a grenade during the War in New Guinea in 1943.) When he went to England and the United States, he "recycled" his old radio concepts. He sold *Dossier on Dumetrius* as a film; titled *Requiem for a Redhead*, it starred Richard Denning. *Walk a Crooked Mile* became *A Mask for Alexis*. His comedy adventure serial, *The Knave of Hearts*, became the basis for a 1963 movie called *Love is a Ball*, starring Charles Boyer and Glenn Ford. *Stranger in Paradise* was published in an American magazine as *Morning After Murder*, and *Twenty-Six Hours* as *The Faceless Ones*. It also appears he wrote other stories for television and magazines. His Gregory Keen stories were translated into about ten different languages including Turkish. Lindsay died in London in 1994.

WHERE did the ideas for shows come from? Some were American. Many were book adaptations or were inspired by books. Oddly enough, writers very rarely gave us ideas; they were too busy churning out scripts to beat deadlines. And often the writers who came to us with their own ideas were not very good radio writers anyway. It was hard to write for Grace because she wanted everything in the first episode. There was no time to ease into the story. It had to start with a bang! There had to be action and conflict right from the start, otherwise station managers just were not interested.

Famous books always ensured a receptive audience. Book adaptations quickly became cornerstones of Grace's output; looking back, half our shows began as books. *Cattleman* and *The Bishop's Mantle* were classics of the genre. I tried at least a dozen times to get the radio rights to *Gone with the Wind*, but without success. Our production manager John Saul and I haunted bookstores, searching for novels suitable for adaptation to radio. John wrote to many publishers without much success. I remember a reply we received from the famous British novelist, Nicholas Monsarrat, author of *The Cruel Sea*. He stated categorically he would not permit one word of his books to be changed or deleted, nor could any additional dialogue be added to his novels.

Book adaptations were a specialised discipline that Ross Napier soon mastered. He kept the best-known characters and any famous lines, but invariably departed from the plot of the book by developing entirely new storylines. He had to, if the book were to work in radio. As Ross explained, "Not all books had key points of action that could be built into the radio serial. Sometimes I just invented something that wasn't in the book, and I'd put that in just to please Grace."

In my opinion, when it came to book adaptations, many Australian writers could not add dialogue, or were not game to. Richard Lane was the worst offender; he could not create fresh dialogue or add anything that was not in the original book. Remember, a long book is made long by narration unsuitable for radio; strip that away and suddenly that long book becomes a pamphlet! That was Ross's strength; he added dialogue to everything he did, even if that meant expanding the original story.

WITH all her great shows running on air, Grace was finally seeing a return on her investments. In April 1952, she bought British Australian Programmes (BAP), and took over their studio and office in the City Mutual Building, 60 Hunter Street. I'm quite sure that the art deco architecture appealed to her American soul. She hired John Woodward from ARC. John had been panel operator when Grace's first show, *Here Are the Facts*, was recorded at AWA. Later, as ARC's senior panel operator, he was involved in much of Grace's recording work. Meanwhile, my despatch department now expanded; it was spread over space in our new office, with three more rooms back in Savoy House!

When Grace first purchased BAP, she retained the name and ran it as a separate entity. The purchase included a number of old programmes produced by BAP. Unfortunately they were no longer saleable and so were destroyed.

GRACE and Ronnie were an enviable couple.

After the War, Ronnie sold insurance before he joined Frank Packer's Consolidated Press as personnel manager, helping British migrants settle into jobs with the company. While Ronnie worked for Packer, he could not join Royal Sydney Golf Club. Neither, in fact, could Packer, because newspaper people were not accepted as members. Instead, Ronnie became a member of the Australian at Kensington. He took me there a few times for a game. (Sometimes he took me to lunch at the American Club. No wonder I worked so much unpaid overtime!)

In public they were Mr Parr and Miss Gibson. When a stranger once asked Ronnie if he was also in radio, Grace laughed and said, "He'd never even heard of commercial radio till he met me." And I think that might have been true. If Ronnie listened to radio at all, it was probably the ABC.

But what kind of a man was Ronnie? For one thing, I am sure that a man of Ronnie's background would have been bemused by his wife's bizarre world of actors and writers. I have always believed that he was sensible enough to keep out of Grace's business. On the few occasions when he did make a comment, she would simply tell him, "Be quiet, Ronnie." Instead, he became the charming figure in the background. He gave Grace the stability she had never really had. They were both very strong people, and yet there was no competition between them.

Later, Ronnie left his executive position with Sir Frank Packer so he could accompany Grace around the world, taking care of the business of making the trip happen, helping her entertain her clients, content to play a supporting role. In that era, when it was difficult for a woman to go on business trips alone, Ronnie came into his own. But he was not an underling! He was the strength behind her. He was the centre of her universe.

Because of her American connections, Grace was able to establish a Hollywood office. We had a special Hollywood label and found a small market for our half-hour self-contained shows. We also had a Canadian representative, and an important one in New Zealand. In 1952, Grace made her visit to South Africa, which was to become a first-class market. From there she flew to England and on to the West Indies. (Others who made trips to South Africa were Donovan Joyce from Melbourne and Artransa's sales executive, Sam Baker.) Along the way, Grace enjoyed visiting her family in America but eventually the trip became too much for her and she settled down to end her days in Sydney.

AS YOU have no doubt gathered by now, Grace was a very determined woman who got what she wanted. But underneath that impassive shell was a mass of contradictions; she could be mean and manipulative, generous and loyal, all on the same day! However, one incident in her life left me wondering whether I really did know Grace as well as I had thought.

She and Ronnie lived in style at *Kings Lynn*, Ithaca Road, Elizabeth

Bay. Its atmosphere reminded me of an exclusive London club, filled with 18th century mahogany and cedar furniture, upholstered in satin damask, oyster and mushroom pink. Old silver and Eastern treasures filled a cabinet. Green leather-bound volumes of Irish history lined a bookcase. On one wall stood a pair of Chinese idols on teakwood brackets; Chinese paintings adorned another.

Then, in 1956, Grace purchased the penthouse at Macleay Regis on Macleay Street, Potts Point. It had all the grandeur of a luxurious New York apartment with sweeping harbour views from the Bridge to the Heads. The palatial living and dining rooms, with their majestic fireplaces, opened out onto a garden patio. A vast kitchen could provide meals for over a hundred guests. There were three large bedrooms, and even the maid's quarters had a private terrace. The price tag: £19,000. However, the deal proceeded on the understanding that she could *not* gain vacant possession for at least two years. The purchase went through.

The ink was barely dry before Grace hired a good lawyer and had vacant possession within *three months*. Basically all she had to do was prove that the tenant — a highly paid executive of Philips — could afford alternative accommodation for the same rent he was paying in Macleay Regis. Immediately Grace paid another £6,000 for renovations and she had her perfect home. Her next step was off to America to purchase her furnishings — mostly antiques. It then became my job to get them through customs with the least possible trouble and expense.

On one occasion, I had to deliver some material to the penthouse. We always used Waratah Taxi Trucks and the drivers were all known to us. This time, though, we had a driver I had not met before. When we arrived at the penthouse, he came in and we started to look around. Grace offered him a drink and he said, "No, I won't, thank you very much." "Oh," said Grace, "you're the *only* Waratah man who doesn't have a drink." It turned out he was the manager of the company!

Grace did a lot of entertaining at the penthouse, and lived there until she passed away. At one stage, Grace and Ronnie debated retiring to Honolulu, but after much discussion decided to stay where they were. The penthouse was eventually sold for more than one million dollars.

Grace Gibson. *"I was ushered into this mysterious woman's office. I knew at once that in some way she was foreign …"*

(Photo courtesy of Commercial Radio Australia)

The voices I grew up listening to: *(Back row)* Reg Morgan, John Dease, Jack Davey, Charles Cousens, and Jack Lumsdaine.
(Front row) Albert Russell, 2GB chief announcer Eric Colman, and Harry Dearth. If Eric Colman looks familiar, he was the brother of movie star Ronald Colman.

George Edwards dominated early radio with *Dad and Dave* and *Inspector Scott*.
(Photos courtesy of Commercial Radio Australia)

Reg Johnston *(lower right)* directing a Grace Gibson show in 1945.
He was the creative soul of the company.

The man who replaced him: Lawrence H. Cecil.

(Photo courtesy of Commercial Radio Australia)

The glamorous 2UW Auditorium — known as the "Theatre Beautiful" — seen from the sponsors' and station directors' soundproof box.

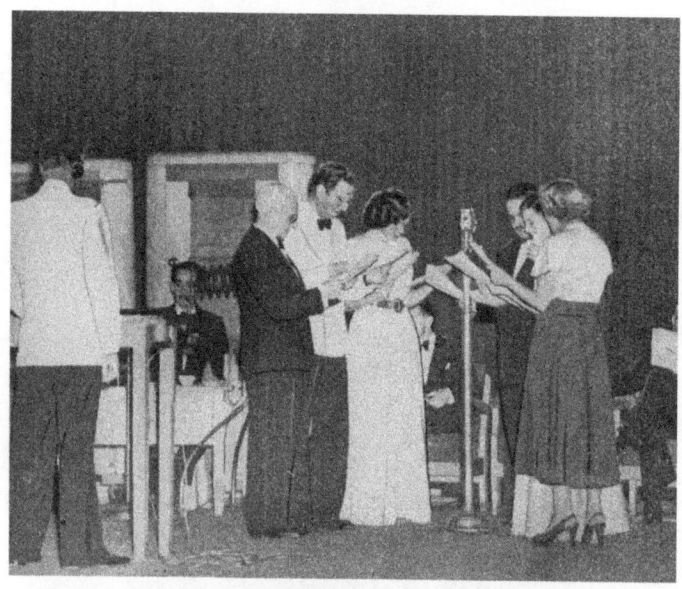

Harry Dearth (in white coat, back to camera) directed the *Lux Radio Theatre* from the stage.

(Photos courtesy of Commercial Radio Australia)

Actor John Saul *(seated, second left)* and the cast from *Dr Paul*. With him in the front row are *(first left)* Michael Plant and *(seated right)* Reg Johnston. Back row: *(from left)* Alan White, (unknown), Neva Carr Glynn, Dinah Shearing, and Ron Roberts. Recalls Dinah Shearing, "Nessie and I, and the other lass, were bunched together on a tall thin table, and Ronnie was actually holding me as I perched on the end."

John Saul was Rod Taylor's mentor.

Michael Pate, one of our early stars.

James Condon in *The Guiding Light*.

Alan White, great actor, great friend.

I can still hear their voices today. *(Above left)* Dinah Shearing, and *(above right)* Amber Mae Cecil.

Sydney radio in the 1940s: The announcing studio at 2UE Sydney. The microphone could pick up sound from both sides so two announcers could work together. It was slung from the ceiling to prevent unnecessary vibration.

The 2UE control room.

The 2UE record library housed thousands of discs.

(Photos courtesy of Commercial Radio Australia)

Country radio stations came in all shapes and sizes.
Above left: the original headquarters of 4GY Gympie.
Above right: the original 2AD Armidale.

The studio lobby of 4GR Toowoomba.
(Photo courtesy of Commercial Radio Australia)

Episode 5

The Great Voices

WHENEVER I am asked to nominate the top performances in our shows, I invariably come up with the same list:

Alan White, *Night Beat*
Michael Pate, *The Bishop's Mantle*
Frank Waters, *Dragnet* and *Cattleman*
Bruce Stewart, *Dossier on Dumetrius*
Dinah Shearing, *Dr Paul* and *Tudor Queen*
Richard Meikle and John Unicomb, *Becket*
Amber Mae Cecil, *Desiree*
Lloyd Lamble, *The Shadow*
Lyndall Barbour, *Portia Faces Life* and *Cattleman*
Ron Roberts, for being such a superlative narrator and gentleman.

For the single most memorable performance in a role, I cannot go past Thelma Scott in *Knock at the Door*, from the *Nyal Radio Playhouse*.

SIR Laurence Olivier once said, "Australian actors are the best sight-readers in the world".

They were able to walk into a studio, pick up their scripts, and immediately deliver an intelligent reading in character — just by sight-reading. It was no small feat, and required enormous reserves of physical and mental stamina. We always allowed one hour in which to rehearse and record each fifteen-minute episode. Only one microphone was used, and the actors moved forwards, backwards, and around the studio as required. Not only did they have to deliver their best acting, they had to ensure that the microphone did not pick up any rustling sounds as they turned the pages of their scripts. And although we asked actors to pick up their scripts beforehand, it was often impossible; they were simply too busy.

At many studios, episodes were "flown" — there were no read-throughs, no rehearsals with music and sound effects; everyone had one shot at it. The pressures were enormous. "Fluffs" — that is, mistakes — were costly in the old days when we recorded straight onto a master disc. A master disc was worth about £2/10/-, which was a big portion of the £25 it cost to make one episode. The master would have to be discarded, and the whole cast would have to start again. If an actor often caused recuts, he or she would not get work. Some of our actors could pick up on a lot of faults, they could pick up from each other, and they were very sincere about their acting in those days. Some fluffs were let through if they sounded natural.

Remember, too, that our typists were only human and sometimes made mistakes. The actor had to overcome these in the moment of recording. Some actors were very adept at covering minor fluffs; others were panic stricken. If an actor fluffed regularly, he or she did not get much work. Word soon spread. Overseas artists who came to Australia had great difficulty working under our conditions. And overtime was *not* paid on actors' mistakes. Fluffs were made, masters ruined, and the actors were late for their next job. Conditions were demanding, but nobody wanted to leave the profession. Of course, once tape came into use, artists tended to lose their sight-reading skills because the pressure was off. Mistakes could be snipped out easily.

BY 1954, Grace had recorded 7,000 quarter-hour shows. She was booking no fewer than 180 casting calls a week. And she was not the only one. The best voices were always in demand, and other studios competed for them as well. We constantly juggled our casting calls; very often episodes were recorded out of sequence to accommodate actors' schedules. The studios cooperated with one another and the actors' agents as best they could. Travel between studios added more pressure to the actors. The most dedicated ones collected their scripts beforehand so they could study their parts, correct any typographical errors, and prepare their characters.

The actors tried to help one another too. They had their camaraderie — what I would describe as "good friendships with some back biting". Most of them got on well, and those that did not probably could not have got on well with anybody.

Peter Finch was probably the best actor to my mind. He appeared in only two of our productions that I recall: a part in the first episode of *The Shadow*, and the starring role in a half hour play called *Till The Day I Die*, recorded in 1946. It was a masterful performance. Grace always believed that Peter Finch was going to be a star. She said the same about Rod Taylor, who died while I was writing this book. When Rod first appeared in shows like *Night Beat* in 1950, he was a handsome young art student yet always oddly nervous in the studio. Within six years of his debut as a raw amateur in Sydney radio, he was appearing with another Taylor — Elizabeth Taylor — in two major movies, *Giant* and *Raintree County*. In 1963 came the starring role in the Alfred Hitchcock classic, *The Birds*. Our John Saul was his lifelong friend and mentor; more about that later.

Michael Pate and Alan White were very good, as were John Bushelle, Frank Waters, Nigel Lovell, and Richard Meikle. Peter Gwynne had a full, rich voice and worked a lot for us in character roles. John Cazabon was a good character actor. He could play up to six different voices in one episode. He typified how versatile actors needed to be.

Ray Barrett was another fine actor. We never "starred" him in any of our shows because he was popping up in so many other shows and commercials that listeners and stations were getting fed up with him. He was so overexposed it was just as well he went to England!

Ric Hutton delivered a perfect performance in *The Castlereagh Line*, particularly so as he hated the character he portrayed. It was entirely against his way of life, but his portrayal was utterly convincing.

Howard Craven was in a lot of our shows, mainly as a narrator, and of course Ron Roberts was the very best narrator radio ever produced. He was very good at sound effects as well.

LOOKING back, I have to say that my two favourite actors in Sydney radio were Michael Pate and Alan White. I met them soon after I joined Grace. Reg Johnston was their friend and was helping them both establish their careers in radio drama.

Michael was cast as star of a book adaptation, *The Bishop's Mantle*. He was superlative. Then he and Alan starred together in another book adaptation, *Escape Me Never*. I was very fortunate to do the sound effects for Michael's final recording session in Australia before he left to work and live in Hollywood. It was a difficult play and Michael Plant was helping with sound effects too. The next time I saw Michael Pate, after he had returned from America, was at the Customs Department where we were both collecting parcels. The moment he spotted me he came straight over and started chatting away as though he had never been away and become a Hollywood star. (In Hollywood movies, he often played a Red Indian, but no matter what make-up he was wearing you would always know it was him, courtesy of his wonderful voice.) The last time I saw Michael was at his home on the Central Coast when Jim Aitchison and I went up to interview him for our book, *Yes, Miss Gibson*. It was a delightful visit. He was a great storyteller, regaled us with many yarns about radio since the late 1930s, and filled more microcassettes than anyone else we interviewed. As a result, we were late for our next interview session with Dinah Shearing and Alastair Duncan. When I apologised and told them where we had been, Dinah said, "If you've been with Michael, you've *got* to be late!"

Likewise, Alan White was a superb actor and a wonderful person. Every Christmas in Savoy House, the Australian Record Company had a large party. Everyone at Grace's office had an invitation but as the junior, I had been left behind to look after the office. Alan White came down to pick up a script and saw me there. He asked what I was doing there on my own. I explained I was just the office boy and had to man the office. Within five minutes, Alan was back with a drink and a plate full of food for me. It impressed me that such a leading actor would bother to do that for me!

On another occasion, when Grace visited Britain, Alan — by that time well established as a London actor — took her to lunch at the Associated British Film Studio's restaurant and introduced her to Trevor Howard. Having starred in *Brief Encounter* and *The Third Man*, Trevor was one of Grace's favourite actors. According to Alan, Grace was radiant that day, while Trevor, a cricket fanatic, was interested in all things Australian to the point of flying out here to see Test matches. That lunch was such a kind and thoughtful gesture on Alan's part, and I am sure it gave Grace enormous pleasure. It was very typical of Alan who never forgot his humble beginnings; he was born in Five Dock in 1924, educated at Fort Street, and worked hard to master his craft. He was a top radio talent, and was also touring in the stage play *Dial M for Murder*, when a British theatrical agent named Elsie Beyer lured him to London.

Alan had an impressive career there and lived in Dolphin Square, a gracious apartment complex near Westminster, wherein each residence bore the name of a British navigator. It was a far cry from Five Dock!

Dolphin Square's many distinguished residents included Prime Minister Harold Wilson; Maxwell Knight who recruited Ian Fleming to join MI5 and who later inspired "M" in the James Bond novels; and entertainers Arthur Askey, Tommy Trinder, Vic Oliver, and Bud Flanagan (of Flanagan and Allen). Infamous subtenants included Christine Keeler and Mandy Rice-Davies. Incredibly, Alan lived in Grenville House that had been the Free French wartime headquarters of General de Gaulle in 1940. If only walls could speak …

One voice Grace adored was that of Ron Roberts. It was a convention that quarter-hour serials always opened and closed with a formal narration. Ron soon became Grace's "house" narrator. He was incomparable. Ron's wife, Hilda Scurr, was a radio actress and an accomplished drama director at EMI. Later, she directed *Dr Paul* and *Drama of Medicine* for Grace. Ron and Hilda escaped the radio rat race every weekend and headed to their idyllic retreat in Bowral. After all my years in radio, I always nominate Ron Roberts as one of the great gentlemen of our industry. He was also very smart. Not only did he get a lot of work because he had such a beautiful voice, he was also very good at sound effects. We could not afford a separate sound effects man, so Ron did them all. It was not about exploiting actors; doing sound effects was fun. If Ron Roberts, James Condon, and Richard Meikle were in the same show, they competed with one another to see who would do the sound effects.

Veteran actor John Saul had a long association with Grace. I met him very early in my career, in 1946, when he was directing *The Story of Flight*, narrated by Reg Johnston, and sponsored by Qantas. Before then, I had heard John in many roles when I was growing up, particularly as Dave in *Dad and Dave*. John was a sympathetic actor with a good voice, and a frequent star in the Macquarie and Lux plays. I also knew his wife Georgie Sterling through her acting in many radio shows. John was a soft-spoken person, very friendly, and always good company. He was certainly one of Grace's favourite actors. He did not commence in *Dr Paul* until about episode 30, but then went on to define the role of the good doctor. He retired from acting very early but directed shows for Grace for many years, mostly our serials during the 1950s and early 1960s. He and Ross Napier worked well together. When Lawrie Cecil retired, John took over as production manager. Like Lawrie, he possessed a ferocious temper. Actors were petrified of him. If someone clowned around, or failed to deliver the effect he wanted, John vented his fury. He was a very pleasant person otherwise, but he had a tendency to brood.

He and his wife Georgie Sterling were both at the top in radio and, more importantly, happily married. They lived at Newport on Sydney's northern beaches. In his retirement, John took up painting and we all looked forward to his first exhibition. I have no doubt his paintings were good, but when I asked him what they represented he replied, "My f-----g guts!" I asked no more, but thought it was a good description. When John passed away, we were not officially informed. Georgie became a recluse for some time before eventually returning to the scene and doing some acting. She was always a welcome guest at Grace's Christmas lunch.

John and Georgie were close friends of Rod Taylor. As I mentioned earlier, John was Rod's mentor. John and Georgie visited Rod in the States several times after he became a big star. John told me that when Rod first arrived in the States by ship he was receiving an allowance for his food. When he handed in his expenses he was told, "If you want to be a big star, you have to spend up big." So the next time the Sauls went to dinner with Rod he ordered by the price. On another occasion, John was woken by a telephone call in the middle of the night. A strangely familiar woman's voice, husky and sultry, said, "Hello, John," but he had no idea who she was. After a pause Rod came on the line and said, "Didn't you recognise June Allyson?" Apparently Rod and June were an item!

WHILE I can easily come up with a list of thirty very good male actors who were in constant demand, I would be battling to get past a dozen names of the ladies. It is a sad reflection of the era; there were limited roles for women. Even the quarter-hour daytime serials were skewed towards male actors, probably because the main audience for them was women. Women were particularly disadvantaged; there were always the leading actresses, of course, but more roles were available to men. On average, out of a cast of six, only two roles would be for women. And only a handful of shows actually starred a woman: *Portia Faces Life*, *Big Sister*, *Delia of Four Winds*, *Life of Mary Sothern*, *When a Girl Marries*, *Sara Dane*, *Tudor Queen*, *Pretty Kitty Kelly*, and *Aunt Mary*. Even a man portrayed *Mrs 'Obbs!* I remember how Reg Johnston auditioned 18 actresses for the starring role in *Pretty Kitty Kelly*. He selected Lesley Pope who played opposite the love interest John O'Malley. Shortly after, Lesley went to England with her husband Syd Piddington who had a "mind reading" act.

Of the ladies, my favourites were Dinah Shearing, Lyndall Barbour, Sheila Sewell, and Wynne Nelson. Amber Mae Cecil was another very good actor. They were all able to "go" from teenagers to very old ladies. Lyndall was great in *Cattleman*, as Biddy the aboriginal girl. Thelma Scott was another excellent actor, likewise Peg Christensen, very reliable and wonderful to work with. Belinda Giblin was very good in *The Castlereagh Line*. She felt she learned a lot doing that show. She had not done much radio and was amazed at what actors like Ric Hutton could do.

As I mentioned earlier, Thelma Scott's performance in *Knock at the Door* was in my opinion the best single performance in any of our shows. She was cast with Owen Ainley. Owen's character kills his wife's mother and she returns to haunt him. I can remember taking people into the office to listen to it with the lights out. It was terrifying. Poor Thelma told me it took her three days to get over playing her role.

Dinah Shearing would probably be my all-time favourite radio actress. She was beautiful, we were the same age, and we talked a lot about her career and so forth. She first worked with Jack Davey, for whom she had a lot of admiration, and he helped her with her career. Dinah was only 19 when she first met and worked for Grace.

I thought Dinah was terrific as Hedy in *Dossier on Dumetrius*, and when she portrayed Queen Elizabeth the First in *Tudor Princess* and then *Tudor Queen*. She started as a naïve 16-year old girl and continued through to become a 70-year old domineering English monarch. It was quite a daunting task. Years later, I played her some of the episodes and she thought she was horrible, which I strongly disagreed with. Dinah said that people often told her they could always pick her voice in a show. She strenuously denies that could have been the case, though I must confess I am of the same opinion. Whenever I hear her voice, I recognise it instantly. Even when she was playing a character part, there was a particular quality about her voice and acting that stood her apart. Of course, after you listened for a short time, you became engrossed in the story and the character caught your attention. One of her roles I most enjoyed was Eleanor of Aquitaine in *Becket*. Dinah was a very dedicated actor, and responded well to professional direction.

WYNNE Nelson was a gifted actress and a very nice person. It was always a pleasure to work with her. Sometimes I think she was never given the star treatment she deserved. She was a latecomer to radio, starting out in 1953 at the age of 19. We recognised her talent at once and gave her roles in *Famous Trials* and *Night Beat*. She was one of the only radio actresses who had a serial especially written for her; Donovan Joyce created *The Woman in the Mirror*, which Wynne recorded in Sydney under Nigel Lovell's direction. When radio drama waned, Wynne switched to voice-over work. She was soon in great demand. With two young children to raise, she managed to rake in a good income working freelance hours. Wynne played in most of our new four-minuters, and starred in *The Castlereagh Line* as Lottie Long. In this role she appeared as a teenager who in the first few episodes kills a man in self-defence, steals a horse, is raped, then becomes involved in a gang robbery and murder. She is the dominant character in this great saga as she seeks to oppose the vicious Jack Seager, played by Ric Hutton. One of the drawbacks of being a success was that Wynne lost a lot of commercial voice work at 2WS; because of her starring role in *The Castlereagh Line*, the station did not want her overexposed.

Amber Mae Cecil, Lawrence H. Cecil's daughter, was another superb young actress. My favourite role of hers was as Desiree, the girl who almost married Napoleon Bonaparte and finished up as Queen of Sweden. It was a part that required her to age from a teenager to a wise but elderly woman who never forgot her teenage love. Alastair Duncan was Napoleon, and Ron Haddrick was Count Bernadotte, who became the King of Sweden.

I can still hear Dinah, Wynne, and Amber Mae as I write this. They possessed great voices.

TRUST me, I'm not being sycophantic. I give praise where it's due, and none where it's not. There were a few actresses who were awful to work with. Not many, but a few. Therese Desmond was one I did not like. She and her husband, actor Edward Howell, had become household names in 1936 starring in 2CH's *Fred and Maggie Everybody*. She came in once, asking for her scripts, and called me Sam. Ross Napier was in the office at the time and thought it was very funny. I did not! I retaliated quickly. I knew that actors always liked you to know their names, so I turned around and innocently asked *her* name. Therese was horrified to think I did not know who she was.

As for actors, I nearly had a fight once with John Meillon at our office Christmas party. (He was squiring Margo Lee around at the time.)

I caught him in our music office, opening drawers in a filing cabinet. I did not think he should be doing that and told him to shut the drawer and get out. He took umbrage and said he was not looking for anything in particular, just seeing what was in the cabinet. For a couple of minutes we were at each other's throats until our mates pulled us apart. I think I was really lucky because I think he would have murdered me. After that, we became friends.

AROUND 15 years ago, we produced two half-hour radio shows on stage at the Belvoir Theatre. It was a charity performance in support of the Sydney station of Radio for the Print Handicapped.

I was producer-director, and provided scripts from Grace Gibson's. All the actors volunteered their services. It was a dream cast, straight from the old days of radio drama: Michael Pate, Dinah Shearing, Wynne Nelson, Alastair Duncan, and Peg Christensen.

Even though people like Michael had not been in a radio theatre for probably 50 years, they just went *bang!* — straight into it. They were magnificent. The ability had never left them. And the beauty of it was, they still loved doing it!

AFTER Grace retired, she gave $10,000 to the Actors' Benevolent Fund. She was quoted as saying, "I decided I'd made enough money out of them to afford it". The truth was very different. She had been very generous over the years to those who needed assistance; she just did not talk about it. (When she wrote a "good-bye" cheque for *Night Beat's* Harp McGuire before his return to America, his eyes goggled at the zeros.)

Grace was a tough negotiator. Her rule was that the producer purchased all rights from artists and writers. They signed a piece of paper to that effect when receiving their pay. Also, the production cost of every episode was very carefully controlled. Casts were kept lean.

Grace never allowed more than six actors in any quarter-hour episode, and one or more of them had to double as minor characters if required — for example, a waiter, taxi driver, or bellhop. If they spoke less than 40 words in their second character, they earned no extra fee. If they spoke 41 words or more, they had to be paid an extra five shillings. Scriptwriters were instructed to prune the extra words. We were not being mean; it was just that money was tight. Besides, more than five or six voices in a 12-minute show could confuse listeners.

The star always got an extra five shillings. In *Night Beat*, for example, the star was obviously the actor who played Randy Stone. In *Dr Paul* it was really Dr Paul most of the time, but in some episodes he was not in the script. In such a case, the two main actors shared the extra five shillings.

In 1946, the stars were paid £1 per episode. If the star did a double, he received another five shillings. Gradually the rates went up. In the 1950s, the star was earning £1/10/- an episode. Those deemed to be co-stars earned £1/5/-; it was the director's decision. Eventually the actors wanted holiday pay, and we finally had to pay them an extra five percent of their fee as holiday pay. Mostly, the actors were very professional and did their best to be early. It was in their interest to do so. For example, if a call was 9 am, and the cast was not assembled until 9.10 am, we had every right to hold them until 10.10 am. If some of the actors had a job at 10.15 a.m. at Artransa or AWA, they would be chafing at the bit to get away. The studios cooperated with one another too. If a recording session was running late, we always rang the next studio and warned them in advance.

GRACE always believed the sky would fall in when the star of a programme left, usually to go overseas. I shared her apprehension, especially when it affected major shows like *Dr Paul, Night Beat, Cattleman,* and *Gregory Keen*. We really agonised over it. When someone like Alan

White was going away, we would ask ourselves what do we do? Do we stop the show? Who can replace him? Would the audience accept a new voice?

I clearly recall disliking the new Dr Paul, the new Randy Stone, the new Ben McReady, and the new Gregory Keen. But after one or two episodes I was happy. Frankly, it was more of a concern to the company than to the listeners. Listeners accepted a change of voice because the first actor had created the character and the *character* was what mattered, not a different actor. The listeners knew when Harp McGuire replaced Alan White in *Night Beat*. They knew there was a difference, they were not fooled, but they accepted it because it was the character Randy Stone they were listening to, not Alan White or Harp McGuire.

On reflection, a far bigger cause for concern was *overexposure*. All the studios used the same pool of top actors. As a result, they could be heard in show after show on the same night and, thanks to typecasting, they were often playing very similar characters. It did not help the industry, and it must have been confusing for the listeners. I mentioned Ray Barrett earlier; not only did he work in so many different programmes, but he also did lots of commercials. I believe the industry should have done a lot more to discover and nurture new voices. Rod Taylor, June Salter, Wynne Nelson, and Amber Mae Cecil were the new voices of the 1950s; there should have been more.

Another issue that studios brushed aside was maintaining *high standards*. Lack of time was the excuse. In its final years, like lemmings speeding to the edge of the cliff, the radio drama business did not seem to care about the quality of scripts or acting. In the early days of radio drama there had been crusading actors and directors. In the twilight years, that passion had evaporated. The craftsmanship was gone. Work was nothing more than a mechanical process. More so in Sydney than in Melbourne, actors were very adept at "flying" serials. As Dinah Shearing explained, "When you worked with the same people for a long time, you could read from a script straight off. You did not have to rehearse because you knew how each other worked."

In my opinion, actors lost a lot of their skill when we started recording shows on tape. Their performance standards became sloppy. They knew we could easily edit out their mistakes and record over them. This fact was brought home to me one morning when I was in the control room. There were eight fluffs in an episode of *Drama of Medicine*. It was a twelve-minute show, but they had to stop recording eight times! It was just too easy for the panel operator to spool the tape back a bit and start again from the offending error. It could not have happened in the old days.

BY THE end of the 1950s, Grace's company was the largest commercial radio drama producer in the British Commonwealth, and second only to the BBC Transcription Service in terms of output. Without a doubt, she was the "reigning queen" of radio serials.

Episode 6

Competitive Edge

AUSTRALIANS loved radio drama and, by the end of the 1940s, more serials than ever before were being recorded. One hundred commercial radio stations were playing 20,000 separate episodes every week to an audience of several million people. I think 2UW Sydney held the record: a solid block of 12 different serials played from 9 a.m. until 12.30 p.m., Monday to Thursday — with more serials following in the late afternoons.

Grace had an impressive cast of competitors.

In Sydney alone, we were up against AWA, EMI, Ron R. Beck, 2UE, Associated Programmes-Towers of London, the Australian Record Company, Hepworth Productions, and 2UW's Fidelity Radio. They all churned out serials! Macquarie produced programmes for its top-rating network, as did its sister company Artransa; Artransa, though, could sell shows to anyone.

Every production house had its own particular style. I believe we set out to be the best; we demanded a higher standard of script and we rehearsed everything. As actor Michael Pate said, "Grace wanted to be better than anything else — Lux or Macquarie or Artransa or 2UE or 2GB. That's why she made a lot of money. Her shows were of a very fine standard." Many of our competitors took no such pains with their recordings. In radio drama jargon, episodes were "flown". There were no rehearsals. Actors walked in and sight-read their scripts in one take. George Edwards and AWA "flew" everything.

GRACE'S company was expanding at a maddening pace. But no matter how frenzied we were, I believe we exercised greater care than our competitors. Excellence was our heritage, thanks to Grace; thanks to Reg Johnston; and thanks to Michael Plant, Ross Napier, Peter Yeldham, and Kath Carroll.

By 1953 we were producing 50 quarter-hour shows a week. Production spread over three studios: our own studio in the City Mutual Building, ARC's Bligh Street studio, and 2GZ Orange's auditorium in Hosking Place, a lane that runs off Castlereagh Street between Hunter Street and Martin Place, from where the *Lux Radio Theatre* originated. Now you may well wonder why a country radio station, based in Orange, needed an elaborate auditorium in the heart of Sydney. 2GZ first went to air in October 1935. It was a fiercely independent station, competing with Macquarie stations in Bathurst and Parkes. Its general manager, J. E. Ridley, wanted to harness national news, entertainment, and sporting coverage for his listeners. He transferred the main studios and offices to Sydney where all the action was, leaving Alan Ridley to handle the local studios and sales in Orange. In 1937, 2GZ's Hosking House operations opened, and were regarded as the best equipped in Australia. The "floating studios" were in fact a building within a building, reconstructed for perfect acoustic qualities with the floors sealed and layered for perfect soundproofing. Three studios, two producers' booths, an audition room and station control room were truly ahead of their time. (Interestingly, 2GZ's breakfast announcer in the late 1940s was a jazz aficionado whose ship had been torpedoed in the Java Sea in the War; he went on to host ABC radio's Saturday morning jazz show that ran for a record 30 years — Eric Child.)

Now I can let you into a secret: before Grace bought BAP's studio in the City Mutual Building, she was interested in buying the 2GZ facility in Hosking Place. If only she had! I can remember the day she asked me to inspect the property with her. She swore me to silence and I do not think anyone else on the staff knew what she was planning. We were both impressed to say the least. Grace even picked out the office that would be hers. I did the same. The studio was large and perfectly equipped. The engineer was a nice person who would have fitted in well with us. Why didn't she go ahead and buy it? I do not know. I never heard anymore about it, and it was not my prerogative to ask the Boss!

WHO WERE the people and programme-makers we were pitted against in Sydney? Many of their names are now forgotten, but the sheer scale of the list will give you some idea of how big and how busy the industry was in those days:

The Macquarie Broadcasting Service was Australia's most powerful broadcasting network with 26 member stations and 35 co-operating stations at its peak. Member stations participated as shareholders in their advertising representation subsidiary, Macquarie Broadcasting Services Pty. Ltd., whereas co-operating stations simply bought programmes of their choice from them. Macquarie produced many of its own dramas, and the big nationally sponsored programmes such as *The Quiz Kids*, *Leave It to the Girls*, and the Jack Davey shows, recording them in the studios of key station 2GB Sydney. Other capital city stations were 3AW Melbourne, 4BH Brisbane, 5DN Adelaide, and 2CA Canberra. I always admired Macquarie for its very strong management; like Ben Coombs, sales director, they were professionals who knew the business and were passionate about it.

Macquarie was famous for prestigious one-hour plays directed by E. Mason Wood and Lawrence H. Cecil, presented from its own auditorium that had opened with a gala broadcast on 18 December 1941. Richard Lane was a "house" writer for many years. Macquarie's broadcasting complex was located at 138 Phillip Street, Sydney, on the site of a house where Henry Lawson started writing in the 1880s. The legendary *Smith's Weekly* was at number 126.

The Major Broadcasting Network was not a company as such, more an association of stations — many owned by influential newspapers — united by common interests. Its 15 stations included some of the most powerful in the business: 2UE Sydney, located on the fourth and fifth floors of Savoy House, and 2KO Newcastle, both owned by the Lamb family; 3DB Melbourne and 3LK Lubeck, part of the *Herald & Weekly Times* conglomerate; the *Courier-Mail* newspaper's 4BK Brisbane and 4AK Toowoomba; the strategically important *Advertiser* network of 5AD Adelaide (producer of the iconic *Yes, What?*), 5PI Crystal Brook, 5MU Murray Bridge, and 5SE Mount Gambier; 6PR Perth, 6CI Collie, and 6TZ Bunbury; 7HT Hobart and the Launceston *Examiner* station, 7EX. Major produced drama, quiz, and variety shows, and acted as a purchasing arm for other programmes.

For twelve years, South African-born Paul Jacklin — a former ABC compere and producer — was 2UE's Head of Production, and Major's National Programme Director. He approved the purchase of such shows as Max Afford's *Danger Unlimited* and *Hagen's Circus*, directed the early episodes himself to establish their style, then handed them over to others. He directed the *Lux Radio Theatre* for 2UE in 1955. When the show ended and radio drama disappeared from the Major network, he joined J. Walter Thompson, the Lux advertising agency, where he rose to become Chairman.

The Commonwealth Broadcasting Network was really only 2UW Sydney and 4BC Brisbane, with a network of other stations cobbled together to suit sponsors' needs. In the mid-1950s, 2UW led an informal "network" comprising 3UZ Melbourne, 4BC Brisbane, 4SB Kingaroy, 6PM Perth, and 6AM Northam.

2UW built a magnificent auditorium — the "Theatre Beautiful" —

in George Street. The building is still there, next to the old Gowings store, and backs onto the lane behind the State Theatre. While not on staff at 2UW, Harry Dearth was its star drama director. Len London did sound effects in the old days. J. Walter Thompson's radio unit employed Len, and I suspect Harry might have been on their payroll too. At one stage, J. Walter Thompson's radio unit controlled the *Lux Radio Theatre* and the *Australian Amateur Hour,* and was nearly as big as George Patterson's radio operation.

Fidelity Radio was owned by 2UW, which no doubt guaranteed them a market for their shows. Their serials included *Big City, The Broken Circle, Candle in the Wind, The Chairman is a Lady,* and *Danger with Grainger*. Fidelity also produced the comedy show *Laugh Till You Cry,* which starred George Foster, Keith Smith, and Ross Higgins; it was performed before a live audience. Most of their shows were on old 16-inch transcriptions that my friend Alf Ward offered to us when 2UW took its serials off air. I would have enjoyed selling them, but by that time stations could not play the old discs.

Ron R. Beck headed the Colgate-Palmolive radio unit. When it was disbanded, he started out on his own in 1951. He quickly established a formidable presence with shows like *Hagen's Circus,* written by Max Afford, and *I Hate Crime,* a raunchy crime show starring Ken Wayne as Larry Kent. We took over Ron's shows in later years, but found it impossible to sell his 30-minute programmes. Ron was a very nice man, and certainly an outstanding producer.

Artransa was probably our stiffest competitor. It was the company Grace had founded. It was part of the Macquarie-2GB family but could sell its shows to anyone; like us, it was very active in foreign markets. It was situated in the 2GB building in Phillip Street, and recorded all its shows there, but made no reference to Macquarie, and I do not know whether it ever produced shows exclusively for Macquarie. By the time 2GB moved to Sussex Street, Artransa had ceased to function.

It always seemed to me that Artransa was left to its own devices by 2GB; it did not appear to have strong management in its later years. The despatch manager was an old mate of mine, an ex-jockey by the name of Bill O'Brien. Artransa concentrated on self-contained 30-minute shows such as *Command Performance, Tower on the Thames, Interpol Confidential, Night Surgeon*, and *Gunsmoke*. Their quarter-hour daytime serials included *We Love and Learn* and *Deadlier than the Male*; and for the kids, over 600 quarter-hour episodes of *Tarzan*, 1,000 episodes of *Superman* starring Leonard Teale in the title role with Margaret Christensen as Lois Lane, and 1,024 quarter-hour episodes of *The Air Adventures of Hop Harrigan* starring Stewart Ginn and John Ewart. I think the kids' serials were their most popular shows. Having listened to all the shows we got from Artransa to resell, I was not overly impressed by their writers or production.

AWA (Amalgamated Wireless Australasia) was a drama pioneer. The AWA Network comprised only one capital city station — 2CH Sydney — as well as 2GF Grafton, 2GN Goulburn, 3BO Bendigo, 4CA Cairns, 4TO Townsville, 4WK Warwick, and 7LA Launceston. Whatever shows it produced therefore had a ready market. AWA's Sydney studios were also hired out to independents; Grace recorded her first show there, and John Hickling from Melbourne also recorded in them.

Their two most famous shows were *When A Girl Marries* and *The Air Adventures of Biggles,* where the adventures in the studio — setting fire to scripts, cutting actors' braces so their pants fell down as they read their lines — were more colourful than any of Biggles's escapades. By today's standards, Biggles was frightfully politically incorrect; noble "white men" were always being hassled by "the natives", while villains spoke with distinctly Germanic accents! Less controversially, Howard Craven starred in their other major kids' serial, *The Adventures of Rocky Starr.*

Amongst their soap operas, AWA produced the very popular serials based on novels by F. J. Thwaites — *The Broken Melody, No Rainbow in the Sky, White Moonlight*, and *They Lived That Spring*. Thwaites was a colourful Australia author who took to wearing a sola topi like the figure on the dust jacket of his book *The Mad Doctor*. Enough said!

From what I can gather, every show AWA produced was "flown" without rehearsal. I did not get to know producer-director Colin Craigen well. Formerly a panel operator at ARC, Jim Manley was another director. Edward Howell and E. Mason Wood also directed there. In my opinion, I would rate actor Allan Trevor as their best director; he was a good actor, and I believed he cared about quality. Their studio manager Ken Johns was a very good friend. Through him, I obtained the AWA library of LP shows for Grace to sell. Sadly, many of their most famous shows were incomplete; dozens of episodes had long gone missing. Overall though, when I consider what they might have achieved given their resources, I have to say they were not very professional.

EMI was the grand daddy of them all. George Edwards (the Man of 1,000 Voices) and his wife Nell Stirling recorded all their company's programmes at the Columbia studio in Homebush, which were mostly written by Maurice Francis. Eric Scott (who played Bill Smith in *Dad and Dave*) was also a staff scriptwriter and producer, churning out such sugary favourites as *Martin's Corner* and *Courtship and Marriage*. Michael Pate once described him as a man totally devoid of humour!

Another scriptwriter, Lorna Bingham, served with Scott until EMI closed down its drama productions. Lorna's credits included *Dad and Dave* (in which her mother, Loris Bingham, played Mum) and *The Search for the Golden Boomerang*. Distraught at the demise of serials and unable to cope with the end of an era, she ran a rooming house in Kings Cross until she suicided in 1968.

Other George Edwards staffers at EMI Homebush included actor-producer Tom Farley and the precocious young actor-writer Sumner Locke Elliott. He spent twelve years with Edwards before writing the iconic Australian play *Rusty Bugles*, and classic novels such as *Careful, He Might Hear You* and *Water Under the Bridge*.

After the death of George Edwards, his former wife Nell Stirling kept the company going until EMI bought it. EMI transferred the unit to its Castlereagh Street headquarters, Emitron House, near Central Station. Tom Farley was business manager, Ron Roberts's wife Hilda Scurr was directing, but the company did not survive for long. Tom returned to acting and Hilda directed shows for Grace such as *Drama of Medicine*. Hilda was such an ebullient person compared to Ron, who had a quieter personality. Another big EMI daytime soap at that time was *The Right to Happiness*.

EMI had always impressed me; they concentrated on good stories, casts, and writers. They seemed to take more care in their work, and I think there was more control over quality. Certainly they had some very good book adaptations; Nevil Shute's *The Far Country*, Jon Cleary's *Forests of the Night* and *North from Thursday*, and Elizabeth Goudge's *Green Dolphin Country*, all adapted by Peter Yeldham. When I started work with Grace, Reg Southey was in charge of EMI Productions. I only met him once when he, Noel Dickson of ART, Ken Johns of AWA and I convened with the Federation of Australian Radio Broadcasters to convince them that radio drama should continue to be broadcast. It was a complete waste of time!

In the early 1970s, Grace took over selling the EMI library. I quickly finalised our arrangement with Bill Ramsey who ran the EMI studios in Castlereagh Street. Bill was a congenial chap who looked after all the stored programmes. Unfortunately, he could not supply their sales lists or any publicity material. (I believe Bill died of a massive heart attack a few years later.) I drove out to the old Columbia building in Homebush and collected all their LP discs; it was a very dirty place.

Associated Programmes-Towers of London did not produce many shows but its most famous was *Address Unknown*, crafted with great skill by producer Creswick Jenkinson, and writers Peter Yeldham and Ross Napier. It is one of the classics of the Golden Age of radio — those tales from the fictional Missing Persons Bureau of London narrated by "Henry Simon" (actor Lionel Stevens). The quality was such that many listeners believed the tales were true! Other shows included *Smoky Dawson* and *Death Takes Small Bites*, adapted from the George Johnston novel, and *Treasure Island* produced for an American company. All their shows were recorded in ARC's studios. Associated Programmes also distributed shows from Towers of London.

But before moving on, I must tell you about the turbulent, charismatic Colin Scrimgeour who founded the company. Scrim, as everyone called him, was a New Zealander and a staunch Methodist. He led a bitter fight for social reform and the rights of commercial broadcasters in his home country. In 1936 he was appointed controller of the National Commercial Broadcasting Service. If the government thought that would keep him quiet, they had misjudged their man. More stormy clashes followed. To silence him once and for all, Scrim — at the age of 40 — was conscripted for military service in the War. In the late 1940s he was "removed" to Sydney! After starting his radio production company, Scrim partnered with Sir Benjamin Fuller and established Associated TV in 1949, which purchased Pagewood film studios. In 1955 Scrim bid for a commercial television licence in Sydney but failed. He worked as a consultant on the development of television in the People's Republic of China; helped the International Protein Organisation investigate new methods of turning grass into protein; and later failed to gain a TV licence in New Zealand.

Now, if you think Scrim's life was colourful, there's more to come: **Towers of London** — and the incredible story of Harry Alan Towers! Born the son of a theatrical agent in Wandsworth, London in 1920,

Towers was a prolific independent radio, television and movie producer and screenwriter. In 1946 he and his mother Margaret Miller Towers started Towers of London, which produced and sold syndicated radio programmes around the world. Towers was highly charismatic and persuasive; the cream of British theatre appeared in his Sherlock Holmes stories — John Gielgud as Holmes and Ralph Richardson as Watson, while Orson Welles was Moriarty. It was a cast to die for!

Many of his shows played in Australia; British actor Clive Brook narrated *Secrets of Scotland Yard*, while Orson Welles escorted us through *The Black Museum*. The latter series began with Welles's sonorous voice: "This is Orson Welles, speaking from London." After Big Ben chimed, Welles continued, "The Black Museum … Here, in the grim stone structure on the Thames that houses Scotland Yard, is a warehouse of homicide…"

Other radio shows boasted such artists as Noel Coward, James Mason, and Sir Thomas Beecham. Bogart and Bacall starred in his *Bold Venture*. Michael Redgrave became his *Horatio Hornblower*. His radio success led to major television series such as *Armchair Theatre*, and the *Fu Manchu* movies starring Christopher Lee, to name but a few.

But in 1961 — in a story straight from a radio serial — Towers and his girlfriend Mariella Novotny, a known prostitute, were charged with operating a vice ring at a New York hotel. He jumped bail and took flight to Europe, making low-budget thrillers in Eastern Bloc countries financed through Liechtenstein and other tax havens. Meanwhile, questioned by the FBI, Novotny claimed Towers was a Soviet agent. More allegations followed; Towers was linked with Stephen Ward, Peter Lawford, the Soviet Union, and a vice ring at the United Nations! Rumours were whispered of Novotny's links to the pre-White House John F. Kennedy. Being an astute producer, Towers knew money solved all problems. He paid a four-thousand-pound fine for jumping bail and all charges were dropped. In 2009, he died in Canada, where he had fled to avoid credit card law suits. I would rank him alongside George Edwards as one of the more interesting, larger-than-life, and flamboyant characters in the business.

The Australian Record Company (ARC) not only recorded, cut masters, and pressed programmes for the industry but also recorded its own shows under the direction of Gordon Grimsdale. He made some good programmes — *Ben Hur, Around the World in 80 Days, Thirty Minutes to Go, Ellen Dodd,* and *Fallen Angel.* ARC had two studios; its panel operators were Ron Wenban, Rod Tremaine, and John Woodward. At ARC, Gordon also directed *Reach for the Sky* and *The Dambusters* for Morris West's company, Australasian Radio Productions (ARP). Apart from ARP, other companies using ARC's studios were Artransa, Hepworth, 2UE, George Patterson Advertising, and of course Grace Gibson.

I was interested to learn recently that ARC was formed in the late 1930s through a merger with an "electrical transcription" radio serial company called Featuradio Sound Productions NSW, which may or may not have been related to Featuradio in Melbourne.

Reg Hepworth operated from a very small office (originally in Sydney's Haymarket, and later at Grosvenor Street near Circular Quay) and recorded some very good shows at ARC's studio in Bligh Street. His serials included *Cleopatra, Dynasty of Death,* and *The Louise Conway Story* starring Lyndall Barbour, Deryck Barnes, Richard Davies, Peter Williams, and John Unicomb. Other popular serials with titles guaranteed to tease his audiences were *The Black Mantilla, Doubt Me Never, Fascination, Hold Back Tomorrow,* and *Intolerance.*

Reg was originally an advertising man, and for 40 years handled the Aeroplane Jelly business. His client, Bert Appleroth, began as a humble Sydney tram conductor who stirred up jelly crystals in his home bathtub to sell on his tram route. His product became so popular that he quit his job and rented out a shed in Paddington for his first factory; a keen aviation fan, Bert believed aeroplanes epitomised all that was modern and exciting, hence the brand's name. Reg Hepworth's first task was to record 5-year-old Joy King singing the iconic jingle "I like Aeroplane Jelly". Joy was chosen from a field of 200 hopefuls and recorded the tune 15 times before the company was satisfied!

Reg was a lovely fellow with a quiet, friendly personality; he carried on his business in a modest, unobtrusive way. After Betty Barnard left Grace, she worked for him for a while. Reg owned some racehorses, and from time to time passed on some very good tips. His last serial was *Cleopatra*. At his request, we took over his shows in the 1960s and he was happy with the results. I was last in touch with Reg in the mid-1980s.

Nora Burnett, who also operated the Telecast theatrical agency, owned **British Australian Programmes**. Grace bought the company in 1952 and took over their studio. I did not know much about their programmes or why they sold out to Grace. Their panel operator was Eden Rutter, whom Grace kept on staff, but I do not think they employed any "name" directors. I believe they had the famous Melbourne actor Arundel Nixon under contract in 1939; he played an acid-tongued bishop in *Joan of Arc*, written by Anthony Scott Veitch. I recall that one of their shows was *Dramas of the Deep*. Without being too unkind, I think it sank without trace.

LOOKING back over that list, you can see we had a lot of very active competitors. Some of them were big companies with deep pockets. But they were only the Sydney ones!

Melbourne was also a very formidable drama market:

Donovan Joyce Productions was famous for strongly plotted dramas with meticulous production that were broadcast in sixteen countries. Don was a big, bearded man with a stormy temper as legendary as his demand for excellence. His favourite writers were Lindsay Hardy and the highly prolific Ru Pullan. Don's arrival on the scene mirrored Grace's departure from Artransa; he controversially resigned as production manager at 3AW Melbourne in 1944, starting his own company a year later. Don's serials included *Office Wife*, *Empty Arms*, *The Lillian Dale Affair*, *Convict Girl*, *The Legend of Kathy Warren*, *Knave of Hearts*, and *The Devil's Duchess*. One of his serials — *Stepmother* — became the precursor of the long-running Markham family saga. He recorded in his own studio, flying top Sydney stars to Melbourne for a week at a time. His brother, James Joyce, was a co-founder of Sydney's Central Casting. He also drove up to Sydney in his Jaguar, or hired director Nigel Lovell, to record shows in that city. Such was his reputation for inventiveness and quality that in the 1950s, the Major Network advanced him £75,000 to develop new programmes. Like Grace, he flew to South Africa and exported a lot of shows to that country. I have it on good account that Don was a great admirer of Grace, both as a marketer and promoter.

He bitterly resented the arrival of television, saying it destroyed his career in its prime. Beyond writing one script for *Homicide*, he made no attempt to use his formidable talent in that medium. Instead he travelled to Israel to investigate a scroll allegedly written by Christ. His book, *The Jesus Scroll*, was a highly controversial best seller.

When Grace did a deal with him to take over his shows, it was a great arrangement. His programmes included the two latest Gregory Keen serials — *Two Roads to Samarra* and *The Smell of Terror*, with which we had excellent sales. Four other good mystery serials included *Stranger in Paradise*, a comedy drama called *Knave of Hearts* that was a little before its time for a radio audience unaccustomed to this type of drama (it was later made into a Hollywood movie starring Glenn Ford and Charles Boyer), *Walk A Crooked Mile* set in England about a gang of thieves disposing of a truckload of loot, and a very different type of mystery called *A Mask for Alexis* — a more serious mystery show whereas the others had been more adventure-oriented, more "goodies and baddies".

Broadcast Exchange of Australia (BEA) was a merger of three pre-War Melbourne transcription companies — Featuradio, Legionnaire, and Televox. Hector Crawford was acting manager and his sister Dorothy directed, until they left and opened their own production company in 1945. Epic serials flowed from its studios: *Delia of Four Winds*, *The Markhams*, *His Heritage*, *Simon Masterton*, and *Lavender Grove*. Madge Thomas, a former actress who first started writing at the age of 53, scripted all the Markham serials. From what I understand, BEA sold their shows to the Major network. They did not have any sales reps out doing the rounds of stations. Later, Grace marketed *Delia*, *The Markhams*, and *Lavender Grove* through the Major Network, but sales were not good.

Hector Crawford Productions was a brother and sister company, Hector and Dorothy, striking out on their own. I do not think Grace knew the Crawfords very well because they stayed mainly in Melbourne. Their police drama *D24*, narrated by Dorothy's husband Roland Strong, dramatised true cases from the Victoria police, and was a precursor to their fantastically successful TV show *Homicide*. They produced serials such as *Dangerous Love* and *John Turner's Family*, and self-contained dramas in great volume: *Here Comes O'Malley*, *Consider Your Verdict*, *Inspector West*, *The Beau*, *No Holiday for Halliday*, and *It's a Crime Mr Collins*. Crime was a profitable genre for them, while Hector relished producing musical programmes such as *The Melba Story*. The Crawfords had strong ties with David Worrall at 3DB, the same station where Curteis Crawford, Hector's brother, was manager. At one stage I believe they represented the BBC transcription library.

Australasian Radio Productions (ARP) was the brainchild of young writer Morris West, who had left the Christian Brothers before taking his final vows. Instead, he learned the radio business and started his own production company in 1945, in a studio over a Smith Street, Collingwood pharmacy. His longest-running show was *The Burtons of Banner Street*. Its sponsor, Bex, insisted on approving all the scripts of its 2,000 episodes in advance; sex, politics, religion, and liquor were out. West was famous for his book adaptations. At his peak, he produced 40 quarter-hours of radio a week, including *Reach for the Sky*, *The Dambusters* (which was narrated by the author Paul Brickhill), *The Great Escape*, *On the Beach*, *Chequerboard*, *Forests of the Night*, *Campbell's Kingdom*, *Elephant Walk*, *City Hospital*, *Dick Barton*, and *They're a Weird Mob*, the only commercially produced serial ever broadcast on the ABC. One of his finest serials was *White Coolies*, the story of Australian Army nurse, Betty Jeffrey, who was captured and imprisoned by the Japanese during World War II. West recorded in his own premises in Melbourne and at ARC in Sydney.

It was rumoured that he only wrote the first episodes of a show and then farmed out the rest to other writers. I have no way of knowing whether or not this was true, but it was certainly a good idea because the characters and plots would have already been established in the first scripts. When West left to write novels in the mid-1950s and later sold the company, its name changed to Australasian Radio and Television Productions (ART). Noel Dickson was then in charge. Grace negotiated to distribute their shows on LPs, and I rated their serials highly — good stories and good acting. Unfortunately, their discs were not in good condition and we had to stop selling them. Now, of course, with modern technology that eliminates hiss and surface noise, Grace Gibson may be able to reissue them.

Former advertising executive **John Hickling** produced 70 radio serials, recording them at the rate of 20 episodes a day in his own studio, often writing them himself and skilfully operating his own panel. By all accounts, Hickling was very accomplished. I had heard of him but we never met, and he is largely forgotten today.

However, his story is tragic, and I would like to share it with you because it mirrors the rise and fall of Golden Years radio drama. Born Rupert John Hickling in 1906, he was the radio manager of the Catts Patterson advertising agency Melbourne, switching later to Goldberg Advertising. By the mid-1930s he was producing radio shows every night of the week for such sponsors as Dunlop and Black & White cigarettes. At Legionnaire he teamed with Hal Percy and produced *Imperial Leader,* an immaculate production tracing the life of Winston Churchill, which starred Douglas Kelly and Catherine Duncan. In 1936, Hickling shot to fame with *The March of Time*, a documentary-drama reflecting events of the time that garnered top ratings around Australia. Hickling set up his own company to catch the wartime boom in radio drama. One of his shows was *The Adventures of Peter Chance*. Postwar though, he found himself battling new competitors such as Donovan Joyce and Morris West. Writers Catherine Duncan and John Ormiston Reid helped maintain Hickling's frenetic output that included dramatisations of crime novels by Erle Stanley Gardner and Edgar Wallace. The arrival of television proved his nemesis. He shut up shop and moved to London, determined to break into the new medium. He failed. He retreated to Majorca in Spain, where he died in poverty and obscurity in 1967.

Respected Melbourne actor **Robert Peach** also opened a production company. Peach had been acting on radio since the age of six. During the War, Peach piloted cloak-and-dagger missions in support of resistance movements in Europe. Back in Melbourne, the boom in radio serials saw him acting in from six to 12 serial episodes a day, many for Morris West. Robert Peach Productions started in the early 1950s, producing serials such as *100 Flowers of Death*, a thriller set in Asia, as well as music programmes. Next, Peach joined advertising agency USP Benson. Relocated to Sydney he later switched to writing TV shows for the ABC before gaining national fame in 1967 as the first presenter of

ABC radio's *AM* current affairs programme.

THE Australian Broadcasting Commission (as the ABC then was) was a competitor, even though our programmes were different from theirs. They were more like the BBC, and the BBC was our main competitor in the West Indies, Fiji, and South Africa to a certain extent. We existed to entertain people and keep them listening, whereas the ABC and the government broadcaster in New Zealand were trying to "uplift" people. They did stories *they* wanted to do rather than those *the audience* wanted to enjoy. The average Mrs Smith would rather a good story like *Dr Paul* and other serials. We once had a long meeting at Radio New Zealand as to why their audiences liked our dramas yet would not listen to theirs. Of course they thought their drama was much better than ours, but again they were talking about subjects that did not particularly interest people. Yes, Shakespeare is wonderful but given a choice, who's going to listen to it on the radio just out of the blue?

It was often said that people who listened to the ABC would never really like serials. I believe ABC audiences, like other audiences, wanted something fresh. Even now at the Bowling Club, people never admit to having listened to commercial serials, then they let something slip and you realise they were indeed fans of old-time radio drama. In reality, everybody listened to drama, even if it was *Blue Hills* on the ABC, which was more directed at rural listeners. As someone once said, "*Blue Hills* stopped the country!"

Classic novels were important and popular, but only a good story really holds your interest. We never thought too much about adapting classic novels such as *Pride and Prejudice*. We left them to the ABC. We mainly produced whodunits for the evenings, and daytime serials for an audience that was having a cup of tea or doing the housework. The closest Grace came to anything "intellectual" was *Till the End of Time*, the stories of the great composers. It was a beautifully crafted series;

occasionally we brought in a violinist or pianist to play the composer's great works. But we were not trying to educate anyone with this show; we were telling the stories of great composers with all their lives' complications, tragedies, and emotions. Interestingly, when that series went to air in the early 1950s, many commercial stations actually played classical music at night.

AT THE height of radio drama, we were all in competition — but at the same time, we were a very happy fraternity. We all talked together as friends, and the panel operators were part of that community.

In our case, perhaps our true competitive edge lay with the standards set by Reg Johnston, with Grace's indomitable spirit, and with our writers. Grace allowed her writers freedom to write as they pleased, knowing unacceptable language and statements would be deleted. This freedom allowed our writers to fully delineate characters, thus assisting in casting and providing a complete picture to the director. Writers such as Lindsay Hardy and Ross Napier provided scripts that needed very little editing. Some writers could not write for Grace. It was Grace's dictum that the last episode had to be as good as the first. And the first episode *was* crucial. It was the episode that station managers and sponsors always auditioned. If the first episode was not full of compelling excitement, there went the sale. Ross Napier, Peter Yeldham, Lindsay Hardy, and Kath Carroll were the bedrock of Grace Gibson Radio Productions. Without their words, ideas, and professionalism we could not have stood head and shoulders above the rest.

Writers were always a problem, not just for us but also for the whole industry — especially when it came to the long-running serials. Kath Carroll was Grace's best at one time. She took over *Dr Paul* after about 800 American scripts, and ended up writing a couple of thousand original episodes. At first, she received a synopsis from the American writer but was soon on her own. After Kath we had a number of writers, but they were only satisfactory at best. Perhaps our writers would have been more creative if the recompense had been better, but in the main very few had the dedication and pride in their work.

COMEDY was our sticking point. In the very early days we made the comedy detective series *Mr & Mrs North*, and then *The Amazing Mr Malone*. The scripts were American and nothing special. Both programmes only lasted twelve months. Yet comedy was a popular genre in Australia; it seemed that homegrown comedies like *Life with Dexter* would remain in the hands of the big networks.

Our first ventures into situation comedy were two half-hour productions, *My Friend Irma* starring Madi Hedd, Betty McDowall, and Alan White, and *Chipper Molloy and Connie* starring Monte Richardson, Connie Hobbs, John Bushelle, and Kevin Brennan. Monte was an American comedian who was working out here. The shows were our versions of the big American hits *My Friend Irma* and *Fibber McGee and Molly*. Both shows were adapted from American scripts. Reg Johnston directed the first six episodes of each before his death. Then we brought in Harry Dearth to direct them; they were recorded in the 2UW Theatre before a live audience. Unlike other directors who worked from the control room, Harry worked from centre stage where he was distracting to both actors and audience. In fact, it seemed to me that Harry was too interested in his *own* performance on the stage to worry about the overall comedy. To my way of thinking, both shows were old-fashioned — they were first produced in America in the 1940s — and the humour was not Australian. They were not successful and ceased after 52 episodes. Even though we had contracts for them to continue, we never tried to sell a further series. We had got our money back and that was enough. (A little trivia: Madi Hedd's father was a good tenor in a male choir with me.)

In the late 1960s there was a news report about a woman in England who had failed her driving test 49 times. So was born *No, Mrs Maddox*, written by Ross Napier and starring two of Australia's best comedic talents — Gordon Chater as the driving instructor, and Ruth Cracknell as his pupil Mrs Maddox. Although we thought the show was good and sold it to South Africa as well, it never became a real hit. I do not think the show amused a female audience; they did not like someone making fun of their driving. It certainly did not amuse Grace!

GRACE set out on her first round-the-world sales trip in 1952 — and her timing could not have been better. Television in Australia was just four years away, and those six months on the road shored up her profits for the next 30 years.

Her first stop was South Africa where commercial radio had just started. Bob Lord of Artransa had provided a lot of guidance to the broadcaster. And Melbourne's Donovan Joyce had also made a sales trip there. Grace's shows, and those of Artransa's and Donovan Joyce Productions, soon dominated that market just as they did in Australia. In the years that followed, Grace Gibson's name would become the hallmark of popular radio drama in other parts of Africa too — Liberia, Nigeria, Kenya, Rhodesia, and Zambia.

From Johannesburg, Grace travelled to London and the head offices of marketing giant Unilever and global broadcaster Rediffusion. Both companies were immensely powerful and important because they bought radio programmes for the lucrative West Indies markets — Jamaica, Trinidad, Barbados, and British Guiana, now the independent nation of Guyana. When it came to building relationships, Grace believed in the personal touch. No market was too small for her to visit; over the years, she and Ronnie enjoyed their regular visits to the West Indies. The Barbados Sandy Lane Hotel was their favourite spot. Nassau in the Bahamas was also considered worth a few days' stopover. As well as being broadcast in the larger markets of Jamaica,

Trinidad, Barbados, and Guyana, *Dr Paul* and *Portia Faces Life* were played in the Bahamas, Montserrat, Belize, Antigua, St Kitts, St Lucia, St Maarten, Virgin Islands, Bermuda, and Panama. Individually, some of these markets were very small, but collectively they produced worthwhile revenue for Grace, especially since her flagship serials ran for thousands of episodes.

RADIO drama was at its peak some sixty years ago. Most of our competitors are no longer in business. Considering that Grace Gibson Radio Productions has just celebrated its seventieth anniversary, our competitive edge singled out our work successfully.

Episode 7

Country Roads

I MADE my first sales trip in 1953. It was a hard journey, driving around New South Wales and up into southern Queensland, from one radio station to the next, carrying 16-inch transcription discs packed in a huge case — my "demo kit". Having heard all the shows, as well as the many discussions during their production, I really did know my product. That gave me confidence in what I had to sell. Then it became a matter of negotiating and closing the sale.

I also made a point of finding out what a station wanted, and what their interests were. I would always look in the local paper to see what a station was playing. Then, on the way to the station, I would listen in to hear what it sounded like.

I always got a good reception when I arrived, not that they all bought shows from me.

Normally I spent a couple of hours at a station, and played them sample episodes of every show available. As a rule, the sales were not clinched on the day. The kiss of death was when you were told, "We'll buy it when we can sell it." They rarely did. I soon learned that if a station *really* wanted a programme, it would buy it and then the sales department *had* to secure a client to sponsor it!

Previously, Betty Barnard had always handled the country station sales. Now Grace had decided it was my turn to hit the road. I was looking forward to going — it promised to be a great adventure — but before I was allowed to leave, I was taken into Grace's office and put through the third degree. She tested me over what I would do or say in various situations, the way a secret service operative might be briefed before being parachuted into enemy territory. In her mind, she was placing an enormous trust in my ability. After all, sales to regional stations were an important part of her revenue.

Grace herself did all the national sales work, and direct sales to the general managers like Stan (S.R.I.) Clark of Macquarie, the Alberts of 2UW, and Alan Faulkner at 2UE. They were her friends, but they also became my friends. They were very good, very honourable, to deal with. And they were very kind to a young "upstart" like me. I respected them, and many other station managers, not just because they bought what I was selling; I had respect not only for their role, but also for the person in that role.

In those days, local broadcasters and entrepreneurs independently owned most country stations. Some owners were truly colourful characters. Their stations reflected the values and issues of their local communities. Today they are network owned. Their programmes are homogenous, fed from city headquarters. But in the early days the country stations had to struggle to survive.

While 2BH Broken Hill was built to look like a radio station, others had to "make do". 2MO Gunnedah was in an old weatherboard house. 2LM Lismore was located upstairs in a building situated on a creek. On a number of occasions the creek flooded and the duty announcer was stranded until the flood was over. This happened at other stations in the 1940s and 50s, but the announcers always saw it through. Stations had small staffs; even the manager was required to do the most menial tasks. One Queensland manager was notorious for sacking staff with only five minutes' notice to get off the premises; when he himself was given the same treatment, one can only imagine how happy the staff must have been.

Financially, too, some country stations had a battle on their hands. I was looking at some old statistics the other day that brought home the point. In 1935, a quarter-hour session on a Sydney station cost its sponsor around £13. In Melbourne, sponsors paid about £7 for a similar deal. Country stations charged leaner rates. If you wanted to sponsor a quarter-hour session on 3BO Bendigo, it would have cost £2/15/-, while you would have paid £3/16/- on 2GZ Orange. For the same quarter-hour on 2MO Gunnedah, you would have had to stump up only £1/2/6.

DRIVING north from Sydney, the Newcastle market was my baptism of fire. Three commercial stations dominated the city: 2NX, 2KO, and 2HD. 2NX was my first stop. I was determined to get up to speed with the prices the different stations had paid, and win as many new deals as I could. But when I walked into 2NX, alarm bells rang. I discovered that Betty Barnard had offered repeat purchase rights for *Frenchman's Creek* and *Escape Me Never* for 5/- an episode. Naturally, 2NX had snapped up both shows. I checked with the office and was told that they should have been paying about £2 an episode in a major regional market like Newcastle. When I got to rival station 2KO, the manager Alan Faulkner also wanted to buy them. Alan was an important customer and I had a tough job placating him. For a while I was given the blame for the situation, which was not fair. (Years later, Grace tactfully dismissed Betty; they had worked together since Savoy House days. When Betty left, she agreed not to work for an opposition company for six months. Immediately the six months were up, she joined Reg Hepworth Productions.) The first station executive I ever took to lunch was Bob Baeck of 2HD. We had pies and potato in a local café. Bob later became general manager of 3XY Melbourne.

On that first sales trip I had no idea how bad the roads were going to be! Once I got across the Hunter River outside Newcastle, at a place called Hexham, the roads deteriorated rapidly and were mainly dirt, sometimes just plain rock. My next port of call was 2RE Taree — 150 kilometres away, and about five hours' drive! I was so late getting there I got no dinner that night; there were no restaurants and the few hotels in the town closed up before eight o'clock. I was starving.

It was a difficult trip for a young man, driving an Austin A40 Tourer, who had never been out of Sydney before. I soon got used to those bad roads and had a wonderful trip, calling in at all those faraway stations. Grace received a lot of positive feedback, so I was soon on my way doing more trips.

My second trip was a real marathon — this time expanding my territory to more stations in New South Wales, Queensland, and as far north as Cairns. The roads were still pretty bad but I managed. I only lost one tyre and a hubcap. However I hit a kangaroo at Sarina, 34 kilometres south of Mackay, and some 300 kilometres north of Rockhampton. Thankfully, the bumper bars were very strong in those days. There was not much damage; otherwise, I would have been stranded in a charming little sugar town where the statue of a cane toad was the famous landmark on the main street. The whole trip took three-and-a half weeks. But those bone-shaking dusty roads still remain in my memory — they were just awful roads. Jack Davey and the REDeX Trials were welcome to them!

On another trip, which was in the company car — a Ford Falcon, owned by Alberts — I hit a kangaroo outside Bourke. The car was smashed up a bit and I was delayed for a couple of days while repairs were made.

AFTER a while I settled down to a regular routine for the country trips. Here's a typical gruelling itinerary:

Day 1 Sunday:
Drive to Newcastle and stay overnight

Day 2 Monday:
Visit 2KO, 2NX, and 2HD, then drive to Taree for the night

Day 3 Tuesday:
Visit 2RE, then drive on to Kempsey and stay the night

Day 4 Wednesday:
Visit 2KM, then drive on to Coffs Harbour for an overnight break

Day 5 Thursday:
Visit 2CS, then drive to Grafton and visit 2GF, and stay overnight

Day 6 Friday:
Drive to Lismore and visit 2LM, then drive on to Murwillumbah and visit 2MW, and stay overnight

Day 7 Saturday:
Drive to Surfers Paradise and visit 4GG, then stay overnight

Day 8 Sunday:
Drive on to Brisbane and stay overnight

Day 9 Monday:
Visit 4BC, 4BK, and 4KQ, and stay overnight

Day 10 Tuesday:
Drive to Gympie and visit 4GY, then drive on to Nambour …

And so on and on and on! I tried to stay overnight in those towns where the radio folk and I could have drinks and dinner. With luck I managed to keep each country trip to three weeks, arriving back home on a Friday so the weekend would be free. These trips were mainly to NSW and Queensland stations. My Victorian itinerary was similar, with overnighters between stations. A few southern NSW stations were also on the itinerary. Usually I visited South Australian and Tasmanian stations immediately after radio industry conventions.

While I was away, I had to make certain that it was business as usual in the despatch department. Fortunately, I had two boys working for me at that time, and in my absence they were tasked with despatching all the transcriptions well ahead of schedules.

Fortunately we did not have mobile phones in those days, otherwise Grace would have been on the line every few minutes. As it was, Grace never worried me when I was a trip. I sent her detailed reports and new contracts, and only telephoned her if it was urgent. After my return, we would have a long meeting, usually over lunch, and she never criticised my decisions.

Victoria was where I really kept an eagle eye out for the traffic police; they were quite fierce down there. Remarkably, in all my trips, I was only fined twice. The first time I submitted a fine to the company I was told *I* had to pay. My response was, "Then I'll drive slower. How long do you want my trips to take?"

THOSE country station managers were the backbone of the industry. They were underpaid and overworked, but stayed because of their love of radio.

I learned a lot about the nitty-gritty of radio in the bush. Norm Spicer at 2PK Parkes taught me the "bitch factor". Norm always asked me, "Reg, has it got a bitch in it?" If I told Norm that a particular show had a great bitch in it, that was it, he would buy it. His philosophy was simple: the hero could do almost anything because he was a male, but a bitch was the most important character — someone his women listeners could *hate!*

Then there were those unexpected and totally unpredictable issues. Grace had bought the rights to the novel *Cattleman* by R. S. Porteous, which had won a *Courier-Mail* book prize. Produced in 1961, it became one of our best-selling and most memorable shows. A family saga set in outback Queensland, it tells how the young cattle duffer Big Ben McReady carved a life for himself through fire, flood, and two World Wars. At the end of his long life Ben is rich, but his family is divided by greed. Only one person has steadfastly supported him through all those years — Biddy, an aboriginal girl. Her loyalty is touching and illuminates the story with a special quality. However, the hero's affair with an aboriginal girl was a particularly thorny issue at that time for country stations. In fact, the worried manager of 2LM Lismore called me to say he had received a complaint about Biddy and thought he should stop playing the serial. While I have never believed in asking listeners for their opinions, on this occasion I suggested it. A few days later, the manager called back to say that the show would continue because "everyone loves it".

In the country, station staff including managers would never miss an episode of *Dossier on Dumetrius*. I remember how the manager of 4LG Longreach, Royston Marcus, and his wife were holidaying in Sydney. They called up and asked whether they could drop by the office to hear the episodes they were missing while away from home. Naturally we obliged, and they sat happily in my office for nearly three hours.

In a less than pleasing incident, Wally Grant, who owned 2DU Dubbo, came to Sydney to see Grace one day and returned a lot of discs. When we saw them, we were appalled. They were in a terrible condition — some of the discs had no covers left on them and there were cigarette burns on a couple of discs. Grace nearly had a pink fit and gave Wally a good dressing down. After that, Wally did not buy any of our shows for a long time. When I visited him a couple of years later, he was still smarting from the incident. He offered to buy a show from me "just to help", and he chose a serial called *Pathway to the Sun*. When he asked the price (I think it was 15 shillings an episode) he asked for a discount. I said, "You don't get a discount, Wally. But if you buy another show I'll give you a discount." "Oh no, no, no," he said, "I'm just trying to help you out. I'll just buy the one show." That was it, but at least he bought something!

BY THE time I became sales manager in 1962, the golden age of radio was over. The big network deals with Macquarie and Major were not being made anymore. And that meant a lot more time on the road, chasing individual country sales.

When I had started in the business, significant sponsors underpinned productions. The soap companies were amongst the biggest. Colgate-Palmolive even had its own radio unit and brought some of our greatest entertainers to radio — Jack Davey, Roy Rene Mo, and Bob Dyer. From time to time there were changes in sponsorship for various reasons. I can well remember Bob Dyer changing his catchphrase "Happy lathering, customers" to "Happy motoring, customers", and on the odd occasion getting them mixed up, but nobody really minded. We all knew what he meant!

Grace was lucky with soap operas because *Dr Paul* and *Portia Faces Life* (to name but two) had originated in America, and their sponsors had the right of first refusal in any overseas market. As a result, the same companies sponsored the same shows worldwide, from Australia, New Zealand, Africa, and the West Indies.

Apart from the multinationals, major Australian companies and brands were also big sponsors of radio shows. In those days, national coverage was considered to be 40 stations; with a bit of luck you could sell a programme into 40 markets — in one contract! For years the big national sponsors had been loyal to us. But when they transferred their money to television, we were badly affected. Take James Stedman-Henderson Sweets Limited, whose factory at Rosebery was famously called Sweetacres. The company, makers of such iconic Aussie lollies as Minties, Jaffas, Fantales, Life-Savers, and Throaties, had faithfully sponsored *Night Beat* year after year. But not anymore. *Night Beat* ceased production in the middle of 1959. The company's advertising budget was now poured onto TV. For another two years, they purchased repeat performances for those stations in rural markets that had no TV coverage. Meanwhile, other stations including 2GB purchased their own repeat performances so, against all odds, Randy Stone continued to be heard well into the late 1960s.

Not all our sponsors were so loyal. With *Dossier on Dumetrius*, the original Sydney sponsor — a motor auction company — wanted to cancel before the show was halfway through. Fortunately, Winn's Stores took over and stayed with the entire Gregory Keen series.

Retail stores such as Winn's were excellent radio sponsors, both in capital cities and country areas. They used a very simple way of finding out if their advertising worked. Just by advertising that a sale would start the next morning, they knew from the response whether people had been tuned in the night before. Then of course, whether by accident or design, a station might broadcast the wrong episode of a serial. A flood of angry phone calls to the station would prove that the show was popular.

In later years, the comedy *Chickenman* inspired all sorts of promotions in the bush. At one country station, the well-known manager invited listeners to draw a cartoon of him as The Feathered Fighter and win prizes. Elsewhere there was the retailer who loved walking down the main street and hearing passers-by call out "Chickenman!" to him and make loud chook noises. I guess he was on the way to the bank!

The most negative sponsor we ever had cancelled *The Shadow* because when he walked into his posh Melbourne club someone called out "Only *The Shadow* knows …" Apparently the ensuing laughter caused him a great deal of embarrassment. It takes all kinds, doesn't it?

Episode 8

A New Adventure — Marriage

WHILE I was engrossed with Grace and radio, I do not think Cupid had a chance to catch up with me. My life revolved around work!

Most of my close friends were panel operators and engineers who worked at the Australian Record Company. ARC was where we did most of our recording; they also cut our masters and pressed our transcriptions. Ross Napier was another friend in that circle. We all played golf at Chatswood. Despite being very competitive, we considered that we always played fair — until Ross was caught throwing his ball from the trees back onto the green. He denied the accusation. On another day, Ross and I arrived on the 18th tee all square. Both our shots were close to the green. Ross could not find his ball so I putted out and claimed the match. Then he finally located his ball, putted out, and claimed the match. We argued furiously all the way home. At work on Monday the incident had been forgotten. (Almost.)

Once I got myself a car, I had more freedom to get around. I still played competition tennis out near Maroubra. I used to go out early to play golf — around 6 am! — then I would drive home and play tennis. After a typical Saturday's sport, I was bushed. In later years, Ross joined Avondale and became a very good player. I went back to tennis.

MY FIRST real girlfriend — Vivienne — came from St Martin's and lived in a street nearby. (In fact, all the girls that my brothers and I knew lived within a three-street radius of the church.) We started going out when she was sixteen and I was three years older. Eventually we broke up, but remained friends.

Sometime later, one of my tennis friends asked me if I would be godfather to his baby and I agreed. (Of course all this happened around the same church, St Martin's.) There were two baptisms that day. We were first and the minister closed the church doors while the next group waited outside. When we came out, there was Vivienne with her baby! The minister's wife, who knew me well and knew all about Vivienne and me, asked her husband, "What's Reg James doing at Vivienne's baby's christening?"

During my illness in 2009, I had an urge to ring people with whom I had been friends over the years. Among them was Vivienne. I discovered that she had been widowed for about ten years and was living in a retirement village only a couple of kilometres from where my daughter lives in Terrigal.

AND then I met Neryl Thomas. She lived in Artarmon, and was secretary to a solicitor.

One of my good friends, Bob Corcoran, who worked for the Australian Record Company, introduced us at a New Year's Eve party. Fifteen months later we were married on 16 March 1962; I was 30, Neryl was younger. As for Bob, he was a flinty kind of bloke — we always argued, and he could be quite obnoxious at times — but he ended up being my best man!

Unbelievably, our wedding day was the day 2UE took its serials off air.

It was a terrible blow and the timing could not have been worse. 2UE and the Major network were a big source of revenue. It made it a very difficult day for me. Grace was present and wanted to talk to me about what the future would be, and to be honest I was not terribly interested at that moment. It was my wedding day — *the biggest day of my life!* — and I did not want to talk business! 2UE could go jump in the lake! Happily, Ross Napier was there and proved very supportive; he was wandering between the Grace and me, trying to intercede, trying to keep us both happy.

As it turned out, 2UE and the Major network did not go back on their word to pay for all the programmes they had purchased but not used. They were a very decent company and would never have done the wrong thing. But they came close to ruining my wedding!

CLEARLY, I had been waiting for the perfect wife. Now I had her, I made sure that work and home were very separate aspects of my life. (On that score I reckoned without Grace, as you'll read shortly.) Only recently Neryl was wondering whether she knew enough about my career. I hope this book helps! She did meet my friends, of course, even though they were work-related. Most of them worked in the recording industry, mainly at ARC, but I was also close to the boys at 2GB, and I also knew the 2UW and AWA people very well. Along with Ross Napier, we mixed together all the time. Neryl came to be part of that social bunch. She also attended radio conventions in later years, and had a great rapport with the station managers. So much so that one night we became separated and I lost her. I eventually found her back at the hotel in a two-up game — not only was she watching, she was throwing as well!

When we got married, I do not think Grace liked Neryl. Grace sensed that now I had a wife, my attention was not solely focused on work. She was very fond of saying things like, "You never used to take holidays, Reg, now you want them *every year!*" Eventually Neryl and Grace grew closer. Neryl and Ronnie Parr got on particularly well.

Adam was born in 1963, Megan in 1965, Christine in 1967, and

Glenys in 1970. I always remember how Fred MacKay, our company accountant, and Ross Napier took me aside one night after Christine had been born and tried to convince me to call her Grace. Neryl certainly did not want to, and I would have been embarrassed. "You're missing out on a wonderful opportunity," they told me, but Neryl and I refused. I thought it was a bit of racket, taking advantage of the fact that Grace and Ronnie did not have children of their own. And anyway, Grace was not silly. However, when Glenys was born, we decided to name her Glenys Grace — a "GG" — which was a tribute to Grace without implying I was "after something".

When our children were old enough, I brought them in to help in the office. Such as doing the photocopying and odd jobs. They loved coming in. I remember one of them telling Neryl in a loud whisper, "Daddy swears at the office." I used to pay them 20 cents a job, plus I had to pay their fare into town. They never got to listen to recording sessions because the director did not really want people in there. Grace was very fond of our son Adam, and did a lot for him. Ironically, none of them showed any interest in working in radio. It was not me who scared them off; I think it was all the awful FM stations they listened to.

NERYL and I are very proud of the fact that she and our children, and now our grandchildren, are "First Fleeters" — descendants of Owen Cavanough (1762–1841), a sailor on the *Sirius*. When the *Sirius* was wrecked in 1790 on Norfolk Island, he met and married convict girl Margaret Darnell who had been brought to that penal colony aboard *The Prince of Wales*. Margaret had been sentenced to seven years' transportation for stealing some spoons. In 1796, when Margaret was a free woman again, they returned to Port Jackson and raised a family. Owen prospered at Wilberforce where he donated the land on which the oldest church in the district was built. Our grandchildren Griffin and Dylan were baptized in that lovely old building, thus completing the circle.

On the other side of the coin, one of my early ancestors murdered a man who trespassed on his land. Oh, well. Thank God for Owen!

BACK to Grace. No sooner were Neryl and I settling in to married life than Grace threw in the first of many complications — let's not mince words — she threw in some dirty big *spanners!*

It was 1964 and Grace summoned me into her office. She had ten new programmes to sell to the New Zealand Broadcasting Corporation, a government-owned institution that had its own commercial network as well as a national network similar to the ABC. And she wanted me to fly over there and sell them!

I knew that New Zealand was a vital market for us — it bought about 90 per cent of what Grace produced. Clearly, a programme might not recover its cost without a Kiwi sale, let alone make a decent profit. Now, if I had been single, a trip to New Zealand would have been an exciting prospect. But now that I was married, it would mean leaving Neryl behind with our young son Adam. Fortunately Neryl understood, so off I went.

On the Monday, before any business was conducted, I had morning tea with the Director-General of the Corporation and met all the top management. It became immediately clear that they held Grace and her productions in the highest esteem. On that first evening I held a cocktail party for about twenty people. The next day the auditioning commenced in earnest; by Thursday I had auditioned all the shows and discussed them with various officials, followed by lunch and socialising every day. From the officials' point of view, having a "visiting fireman" like me in town was something to look forward to; I do not think they were paid that well, and my presence ensured lots of opportunities to be wined and dined for a week. At that time, there were not as many restaurants in Wellington as there are today, and I did my best to make a good impression. Then I discovered that the network sales manager, arguably the most important executive I was dealing with, loved oysters. It took the rest of the week for me to find a restaurant that sold oysters. On Friday we went there for lunch. He ordered two dozen oysters. That was all he wanted to eat. Then we all went back to the office to learn which shows they were going to purchase. Fortunately for me, they bought all the shows I had auditioned. So it was a very happy Reg who got on the plane to fly home and report to Grace the following Monday.

One of the shows I set out to sell was *Captain Kremmen of the Space Corps*. It starred British comedian, radio DJ, and television entertainer Kenny Everett, who also wrote the very surreal, Spike Milligan-style script. Everett took the name Kremmen from a record label owned by Mel Blanc's son. In the show, Captain Elvis Kremmen has bionic veins, a bionic left foot with a detachable big toe that converts into a space cannon. According to the opening narration, "He has muscles in places where most people don't even have places". Everett always loaded his shows with sexual innuendos. (Example: two men arguing; one says, "I'll have you know I'm a country member," and the other replies, "I know you are.") Everett was sharp; he knew how far to go without being thrown off air. (He was very pally with Freddy Mercury of Queen, and died of AIDS in 1995.) The first manager who heard the show was very excited about it and telexed all his colleagues not to miss buying it. My elation was nipped in the bud when another manager, in the deep south of New Zealand, telexed back to his colleagues, warning them not to buy this dreadful show. I was at a loss for words until I learned he was a born-again Christian and thought the show was "too sexy". Eventually we met face-to-face, and he did not treat me as badly as I thought he might. Even though he realised his error in telexing his opinion, his was the only station in the network that did not play the show.

We actually had a representative — Ken Elliott — selling our shows in New Zealand. When he was killed in an air disaster on his way to

Singapore, we were advised to use Donovan Joyce's rep, Wyn Roberts. I met with him, a man in his sixties, and I was not impressed. I introduced him to our contacts at NZBC and he used to pay them a monthly visit. They did not like him either. Then a friend at the New Zealand Broadcasting Corporation asked me, "Why do you need a sales rep, Reg? Just come over yourself."

From that moment on, New Zealand was my territory.

Episode 9

Up, Up, and Away

ON THE eve of my next holidays, Grace sprang a trap. She wanted me to go to South Africa, where television had yet to begin. The government's South African Broadcasting Corporation ran a commercial radio network, Springbok, which was a prime market for radio drama. Lever Brothers were sponsoring two of our serials there — *Dr Paul* and *Portia Faces Life*. The SABC bought a lot of half-hour shows such as *Night Beat* and *Address Unknown*. They also had a love affair with Willie Fennell's *Life with Dexter*, which must have been played there at least five or six times! Our key competitor was Artransa, because their accountant Bob Lord had been sent there to help start the commercial broadcasting service. Kenya, Rhodesia, and Zambia were also key customers. The more sales Grace could secure, the easier it would be to offset losses in Australia. The timing was crucial.

As far as Grace was concerned, the matter was settled. "If you don't go to Africa, Reg, you can't have your holidays."

I patiently explained that Neryl and I had everything planned. "I've got to have my holidays. We've booked in, we've paid our money, and we're going."

Grace fixed me with her determined gaze. "You've changed, Reg. Before you got married, you never used to take holidays."

It was a stalemate. When Grace and I were mad at each other, I would go into my office and she would go into hers and we would not talk for a week. Finally she compromised. She promised me that Neryl and I could have our holiday if I agreed to go to South Africa at whatever time the South Africans deemed convenient for them. Fair enough, I thought, forgetting how devious Grace could be. A few days later came the news: they had requested that I visit them in February, right when Neryl and I were going on holidays. Now, in retrospect, I'm quite convinced that Grace called them, or sent them a secret telex, suggesting February. At the time I had no choice but believe her. Today, I do not think I would.

So I packed my bags, said goodbye to my disappointed wife, and went to Africa on a lumbering DC6. My itinerary: Johannesburg, Pretoria, Capetown, East London, and Durban, and then on to Nairobi, Rhodesia, and Zambia. On the way, I stopped off in Adelaide and Perth. (In Perth, I sold 6IX two new serials, which covered the cost of the trip!) In typical fashion, a victorious Grace never compensated me for my forfeited holiday payments.

Perth was one thing; South Africa was a different matter. They were loath to make quick decisions, and only fresh new programmes caught their attention. Apartheid was still in place. For the first time in my life I had to be careful that I sat in the right seats, used the right drinking fountains, and entered my hotel through the right door. It was a very strange experience.

So was my visit to Kenya. I was not sure whether I even had a hotel room for the night; the booking agent in Johannesburg could not get through to his counterpart in Nairobi. I arrived at midnight and fortunately did have somewhere to stay; they did not mind accepting money or Australian visitors. Despite it being another memorable experience, I observed a lot of poverty around me. The local Kenyans were very happy to work in the South African mines. Apartheid did not deter them; they could earn a lot more money in South Africa and bring it home to their families. Not only did I sell our recorded programmes in Kenya, I sold the scripts for a number of our shows for translation into Swahili. Apparently it was necessary for the Kenyans to use two translators, so one could check on the other!

AND that was just the beginning. My second trip despatched me to the four corners of the world, selling our programmes and consolidating our grip on those markets. The boy from Daceyville was a latter day Kingsford Smith; up, up, and away.

Thanks to Grace, my itinerary grew longer and longer. Not only would I be going to Johannesburg in South Africa, but I would also fly from there to Rhodesia, London, Chicago, New York, Bermuda, Trinidad, Guyana, Montserrat, Antigua, St Kitts, Puerto Rico, the Virgin Islands, Nassau, Houston, El Paso, Los Angeles, Hawaii, and Wellington! (On the little detour to El Paso, I stayed with Grace's sister and brother.)

It was going to be a three-month trip, which at that time with four young kids was pretty rugged. Neryl was patient about it all; she did not like it, but she knew I had to go if the company were to survive.

During my visit to the West Indies, stations repeatedly told me that they had already broadcast some of the shows I was selling. Eventually, the penny dropped. Our American representative was not reporting all his sales. Grace did not have faith in some of her countrymen and commented, "When they receive money they throw it up to the ceiling. If it stays there, they will send it to you."

Likewise, in the mid-1980s, Grace received a letter from an old friend in America saying how nice it was to be listening to some of her programmes on the huge CBS Network. Grace rang me, asking if we were selling our old dramas over there. I told her we were not, and then contacted CBS. It turned out they had purchased the shows from an old representative who had not been active for us for fifteen years.

We eventually got our money, but I wondered how much more we had lost over the years.

When I was in the West Indies, the Rediffusion stations were a prime market. Rediffusion offered what at first might sound like a bizarre service: it provided listeners with *wired* wireless! The company had opened the first cable radio service in Hull in 1929, where traditional radios could pick up only weak broadcast signals. Initially the service consisted of rebroadcasts of BBC Radio, which was reflected in its trading name: "Rediffusion" simply means "broadcasting again". Soon, Rediffusion developed its own programming from its own studios, and followed the British Empire across the world with its cable radio service. The first British colony to have Rediffusion was Barbados in 1934, and Malta a year later. After the Second World War, Rediffusion expanded operations to Hong Kong, Singapore, Malaysia, Thailand, and Jersey. Rediffusion Singapore, for example, was a powerful competitor to government radio: it boasted a multi-lingual service broadcasting by cable from purpose-built studios with its own auditorium. Later, Rediffusion UK won the coveted London TV weekday television franchise. The company also branched into television sales and rental, computers, and aircraft simulators. By the 1980s, Rediffusion's cable operations were left behind by the new generation of cable TV networks and the entire company was broken up and sold off.

At the time of my visit, British expatriates, or Brits who had been born in the West Indies, were still managing some of the stations. The Rediffusion stations in Trinidad and Barbados were managed by delightful men — old British colonial types — who reminded me so much of Ronnie Parr. I was impressed by their knowledge of their markets and how much they liked Grace from her earlier sales visits. I had a wonderful time there.

In Trinidad I worked every morning, had lunch, and returned to the hotel swimming pool for the rest of the afternoon. In Kingston,

Jamaica, I went to lunch in a very old pub with a delightful beer garden. I was told that this was where the British Admiral used to sit and watch the ships as they came into the harbour. When a pirate ship approached, he was up and off to his ship and after them. It was a lovely spot to while away time. It would have been so much better if Neryl had been able to enjoy it with me.

In Montserrat, the manager of the station was French, hence it was difficult for us to communicate. My pidgin French must not have been that bad because he agreed to broadcast *Portia Faces Life* and *Dr Paul*. In Nassau, I was driven around the island. There, one could swim in the harbor where all the cruise ships berthed. At dinner I learned to drink Margaritas. The exotic concoction of tequila, Cointreau, lime or lemon juice, with salt on the rim of the glass, was a real change from Aussie beer. They suggested I order the Aussie lamb that was on the menu. "No way," I declined. "For what you're charging for a lamb dish here, back home I could buy the whole lamb!"

I rarely left the hotel in St Kitts. I was always driven from the hotel and back after appointments. It was a very small place and I was content to sit on the terrace and watch the crowded ferries leave for the neighbouring island.

My biggest regret about my trip to the West Indies? It did not coincide with a test match. However my hosts made sure I saw the test grounds in Barbados and Trinidad, and I was taken to see Sir Frank Worrell's grave and monument. How those people revered their legendary cricket skipper.

POLITICS frequently governed my dealings with African clients.

I developed a soft spot for Rhodesia, and never saw evidence of apartheid in that country. There were no restrictions against people of colour; a person of any race, provided they were decently dressed and had money in their pockets, was welcome in clubs, hotels, and so forth. I remember many nice experiences with both black and white Rhodesians. My broadcasting contacts there became good friends and impressed me as decent people. When the white-controlled government declared its independence from Britain, international sanctions were placed against Rhodesia. It was devastating. That meant our programme sales were embargoed, and our friends were on their own. Then we began receiving mysterious unexplained payments from South Africa. Discreet enquiries revealed that South Africa was sending our discs to Rhodesia and our friends were remitting payments through that country back to us. After Rhodesia became Zimbabwe, we only sold a few shows to the new Zimbabwe Broadcasting Service. *The Castlereagh Line* was the last. The country was in a bad way, moneywise. Unfortunately, we never again heard from our Rhodesian friends. As many white Rhodesians moved to Australia, perhaps some of them are still with us and also recalling those days.

Zambia gained its independence in 1964. Previously Northern Rhodesia, our shows travelled there by train via South Africa. White people with a strong connection to England were still running the radio service. My visit there was only short; I cannot recall selling any programmes but enjoyed my brief stay.

Sadly, post-independence Kenya had no money for our programmes. They could only afford to buy scripts.

While I felt comfortable in Rhodesia, I never felt truly safe in South Africa. I loved Durban, Pretoria and, of course, Capetown. In Johannesburg, though, the blacks came into town every Sunday dressed in their best clothes and I was advised to be careful.

I have always suspected that Grace had an antipathy towards coloured people, and that was why she stopped travelling to Africa. As the old colonial era gave way to more enlightened times, she would find herself coming into closer contact with black people. Ronnie would not have been concerned, but she was. She once said to me that if she walked into a restaurant or theatre and saw a black man there, she would walk out. It struck me as strange because she was born in El Paso, just on the border of Mexico, and she had Mexican blood in her veins. Her father had been in the Ku Klux Klan, so maybe she had absorbed some of his white supremacist views. I know in later years, under Ronnie's influence, she changed her opinions about coloured people, but in the early 1960s she was happy to leave African trips to yours truly.

And just on the subject of foreign sales: I can look back on clinching many deals, but the one fish that got away was the BBC. I tried to sell them *Dr Paul*. How I tried, time after time. Once or twice I got close to a deal, but sadly it was never to be.

PEOPLE liked saying Grace was stingy. They accused her of exploiting her staff. In light of the way she dealt with my holidays, how could I disagree? But there was more to Grace than met the eye. When you least expected it, she would show how much she cared about people.

After Neryl and I married, we lived in a flat for a few months, then bought our first home at Artarmon. We stayed there a couple of years before looking for something bigger and better. In 1969, when we purchased our home in Pymble, Grace insisted on seeing it. I think she wanted to make sure we were investing in the right property, and Grace was always shrewd in such matters. So up we went with Grace, her visiting brother and his wife, and Fred MacKay the accountant. It was a real "family" occasion. Grace gave the house her blessing.

Funnily enough, while she was there, she noticed the large storage area underneath. It was not long before she mentioned that the company needed more space to store our recorded scripts. Neryl and I agreed, and they were brought to our home. Grace had a power point installed along with a fire alarm. (Many years later, all the scripts went to the National Film and Sound Archive in Canberra.)

Neryl and I were so lucky to buy that house. The vendors' daughter told her parents they should drop the price because the house did not have a double garage, otherwise Neryl and I could *never* have afforded it.

The vendors — a retired accountant and his wife who were downsizing to an apartment in Wollstonecraft — were delightful people. They sold the house to us on condition that we would leave the garden exactly as it was, and that we would not carpet certain rooms because the floors boasted a rare timber. They gave us a lot of help. When we moved in, they introduced us to the minister at the local church, St Swithun's, where Adam and Glenys were later married. It was a very heart-warming experience.

Episode 10

Uncertain Times

WHEN television came to Australia, I was 27. I had spent the first ten years of my working life with Grace, I loved the radio drama business, but now everyone said that the industry — even radio itself — was doomed. It seemed impossible to me that our company would close down. I put my faith in Grace. Against all the odds, I knew Grace would survive.

LONG before television reached Australia, Grace had plans to be part of the new medium.

She changed our business name to Grace Gibson Radio & Television Productions in the early 1950s. Intending to become involved in the new industry, she produced a pilot half-hour drama titled *I Found Joe Barton* starring Bud Tingwell. Despite good reviews, the venture did not pan out. A short time later she formed another company called Grace Gibson Distributors. Its purpose was to sell other company's programmes. The first were half-hour dramas such as *Box 13* with Alan Ladd, and *Bold Venture* with Humphrey Bogart and Lauren Bacall. The 16-inch pressings were so poor that we ceased selling them. Grace Gibson Distributors proved cumbersome so we reverted to Grace Gibson Radio Productions and quietly dropped "& Television". We decided to focus on what we did best.

Meanwhile, Grace knew her old friend and mentor, Sir Frank Packer, was after a licence. Sir Frank was a press baron who had never owned a radio station, and had no knowledge of, or experience in, broadcast media. Grace helped him in many ways with his application for a television licence. She took a great interest in the public inquiry into television. She sent me to the hearings in Sydney and Melbourne when she thought there was an interesting topic, and I would report back on what was said. If Grace needed more information, I would have to go and get the transcript of that topic.

She had lots of pilot films sent out from America for him to view. She came to an arrangement with him that she would import all the programmes and supply them to the stations; in other words, history would repeat itself — Grace would represent Hollywood programme makers in much the same way she had represented the old radio transcription houses. She even secured the Australian rights to *I Love Lucy*, and devised audience participation shows and panel discussions long before Reg Grundy did.

However, it all came to nothing. Once he was awarded the television licence for Channel 9 Sydney, Packer got together with the other licensees and they issued an edict that they would only buy programmes directly from the producers.

Even before the first flickering images graced our homes, Grace was out.

And while she met the Packers occasionally at social functions after that — Grace was friendly with Sir Frank's wife — the blow left a heavy impression.

TELEVISION *was* a big problem, although not as serious as many people initially thought. In fact, radio programme sales actually boomed for a while in the late 1950s. The big national shows survived for another four years. Not all Australian markets had television; sales of drama to metropolitan and country stations continued.

Meanwhile, export sales reached a record high; in 1958, overseas sales of Australian radio dramas were worth over US$1.25 million a year. No one seemed to realise just how big and important the industry was. To my mind, it was an industry worth fighting for and saving.

The industry enjoyed a sense of false security — for a while. When the bubble of the late-1950s boom finally burst, countless thousands of episodes of old radio shows were sold off and melted down as aggregate for new expressways.

Yet, right through to the 1970s, there were still golden opportunities to sell new shows. 2UE had given up serials in the early 1960s, but in the 1970s began playing our shorter duration serials again. And ironically, when each show finished on 2UE, they were then usually played on 2GB. And when 2UW stopped broadcasting *Dr Paul* and *Portia Faces Life*, we sold them to 2CH. There was always drama on the air — if you were prepared to have a go!

Despite this, Artransa gave up the ghost. Spooked by television, AWA and EMI gave up the ghost even earlier. What they had not considered was that a vast country audience was still glued to radio. In fact, places like Darwin did not get television until the *1970s!* In South Africa, there was no television whatsoever at this time. New Zealand got television much later than Australia — mostly in the 1970s. In the West Indies, some islands are only getting it now.

AFTER television got going, times definitely got tougher. But a cool head and a good knowledge of broadcasting basics never went amiss. Bold decisions also pushed the envelope.

If I had learned one thing from all my travels and all my exposure to radio stations of every stripe it was this: The success of a show was always helped when they were broadcast on a good station that placed them in an appropriate timeslot. This is still the case now. Timing is everything. 2UE had Top 40 before they stopped playing dramas. They also broadcast featurettes — or what we call "capsules" — short little segments about all sorts of things. *And* they had Bob Rogers. Our short lifestyle segments suited their new magazine-style format, and Bob Rogers liked the shows, which helped too.

It was John Laws who had the inspired idea to bring *Dad and Dave* back to air on his talkback show. It was an unlikely combination — an old George Edwards serial from the 1940s, in the midst of contemporary talkback — but it worked. Why? Probably because Laws himself was an Australian icon, and reviving another radio icon was acceptable to his listeners. Laws proved that radio drama was *not* only for old people; a good story will always have mass appeal and age does not matter, given the opportunity to listen. There has always been a need for drama. *The Castlereagh Line* certainly proved that.

The problem was, so many of the young, so-called "smart" programmers who went to America to learn about broadcasting trends totally dismissed drama. Their vision was blinkered, their thinking locked into the same formulaic programming. Then there were the station managers who did not want to spend money, or who did not have the staff and skills to find suitable sponsors to cover such costs. Am I starting to sound like an old dinosaur? Possibly, but I have seen what happens when adventurous broadcasters buck the trends and turn the industry on its head!

At the opposite end of the spectrum were stations that wanted drama but did not offer the right vehicles to play it. I remember, not so long ago, an executive at 2UE telling me he wanted to revive *Dr Paul* in a morning timeslot. I tried to find the most exciting episodes I could, but you cannot just put a programme like that to air in isolation; besides, the type of dramas listeners want now is different. He had the best intentions, but I knew it would not have worked and was not surprised when the station did not go ahead.

When the Albert family bought Grace's company, they considered changing the format of their Brisbane station, 4BC, to drama. I was asked to prepare a paper on the programmes that were available. I went through the exercise for our boss, Ian Renton, who was clearly opposed to the idea. Much to everyone's surprise, I agreed with him. They all thought I would be in favour of it because radio drama was my business. But my business was ensuring that when radio drama went on air, it was accepted and enjoyed, and got *further* sales. I did not believe that a modern audience would listen to swathes of old, slow-moving shows; 1950s drama in 1980 would not work. We could not force listeners to listen. I knew the venture was doomed to fail, and if it had gone ahead, it would have delivered a deathblow to radio drama once and for all.

The fact is, *The Castlereagh Line* succeeded because it was a *different* type of radio drama. And it was tried on a new audience in Sydney's Western Suburbs, an audience that was listening out for something different. Keith Graham, then general manager at 2WS, knew it would work because it was a local Australian story that people could relate to — whereas the old shows like *Dr Paul* and *Portia* were set in "Nowheresville"; they were not from anyone's backyard and had a remote quality, so audiences today could not relate to them.

However, Keith's programme staff considered that a six-minute episode of *The Castlereagh Line* was too long; they believed listeners would "tune out". Instead, they argued for a commercial break in the middle, but I stuck to my guns. Six minutes or no sale! Keith let them have their head, and it was twelve months before Ray Bean purchased the show for the station. It also took New Zealand a long time to realise the potential of this entirely new drama. Meanwhile, the smaller country stations immediately grasped the show's potential and quickly put it to air. As they say, the rest is history.

GRACE was determined to stay in business. Many of us wished she would go into television and follow the example of Hector and Dorothy Crawford, but she refused point-blank. Her early foray into television production had left her discouraged. As far as she was concerned, why should she suddenly throw away all her money on TV shows that might, or might not, succeed? In my opinion, if Reg Johnston had survived, we *would* have been in television. He had the drive. I think in those later years that Grace basically kept the company going for the staff.

Grace's first survival strategy was clever. She switched the long-running shows onto "continuing" contracts. This meant that stations could not just phone up and cancel them; they had to give three months' notice of cancellation in writing. When a show ended ahead of time, some stations just let the story stop unfinished, leaving their listeners in the lurch. Other stations were more considerate; they negotiated with us for a special closing episode to be written and recorded, so that the story could at least be resolved before it was taken off air.

Next, Grace took over selling programmes for her competitors. It was an absolute masterstroke that saw her controlling most of the radio programmes that had ever been made in Australia, distributing the libraries of Donovan Joyce, AWA, EMI, Artransa, BEA, and ARP around the world. The first competitor Grace approached was Donovan Joyce. I think he thought we were stupid. A lot of his programmes were still on 16-inch transcriptions, which we had to transfer to tape. But because we had ready overseas markets, we did well out of them. The EMI and ARP libraries offered Grace the best resale opportunities. They also had to be transferred to tape for distribution. It was all worth the effort.

But all of the above was nothing more than a Band-Aid. Yes, we had a new revenue stream, but at best it was a "recycling" exercise. By the early 1960s we realised we had to diversify to meet new broadcasting challenges. As far as radio was concerned, television had taken over the drama audience. The day of news, talkback, and music had not only arrived — it was here to stay. Most of our competitors were parts of larger organisations such as AWA and EMI, and could simply be closed down. But Grace had nothing else to fall back on so it was a case of sell programmes or go broke.

The first decision we made was to develop new, shorter-length, faster-paced dramas, geared to modern radio formats and busy audiences with shorter attention spans. The second was to import fresh new shows from around the world.

WE DEVISED a new radio drama concept: the mini-drama, a serial broadcast weekly in five *four-minute episodes*. Grace believed three minutes was too short for a drama, but in four minutes enough of the story could be developed. She had planned to adapt and shorten old scripts from *Night Beat* and her courtroom dramas, but Ross Napier persuaded her otherwise. Ross maintained that only original stories, specially conceived to work in the new format, would do the job. He was proved right.

On 11 October 1971, the first four-minute Grace Gibson mini-drama went to air on 2UE. Not only was a new drama on air in the Sydney market, but 2UE broadcast it on the top-rating Bob Rogers show. It proved so successful that in 1985, 2WS played a repeat performance.

I Killed Grace Random was the story of a hit-and-run accident based on Elleston Trevor's book *Billboard Madonna*. (Trevor was a big-name author at the time; *The Flight of the Phoenix* had become a major movie.) Richard Meikle starred as an advertising executive who runs down a woman in his car. June Salter and Ron Haddrick co-starred. I'll never forget my slip of the tongue at a meeting; I called the show *I Killed Grace Gibson* — Grace was not amused! When launching it, we supplied publicity shots of our Grace inspecting smashed cars at the NRMA in Parramatta. We also suggested that stations could promote road safety with a "Day of Grace" — a dedicated safe motoring event on the day the show concluded in their market, supported by local sponsors, but the idea did not get enough support. Only 2LF Young took up the idea. The other stations could not be bothered, or could not find the appropriate sponsors.

Every word counted in our new four-minute serials. Their continuing stories each ran for 130 suspense-packed episodes. *I Killed Grace Random*, *My Father's House*, and *Without Shame* defied all predictions, playing in every capital city as well as a vast country network.

The 1973 mini-drama, *We, The Wicked People*, broke more new ground. Ross Napier crafted a complete story weekly in five four-minute episodes. It ran for 260 episodes, enough for a year's airplay. *Before the Court* was another mini-drama with stories self-contained within five four-minute episodes. Next, Ross wrote *Without Shame*, the story of Judith Farrow, a woman whose husband makes love to her sister, the husband and sister are murdered, she gets the blame, and is sent to prison. And all that happens in the first *five* episodes! Once Judith was in gaol, Ross planned to introduce a lesbian warder into the story. When I bounced the idea off 2GB manager Percy Campbell, he turned white and said no. Later, with Ross pioneering the new genre, we moved from four to six minute episodes. He felt four minutes was not quite long enough to keep a story going.

OUR second strategy was to introduce overseas programmes to our markets. We sourced programmes from America, England, Canada, Scotland, New Zealand, and South Africa, providing us with a variety of good shows that our audiences enthusiastically accepted. Grace still had good connections in her homeland and that was where we started our search — we went to the big American networks such as ABC, NBC, and RKO, as well as independent producers. Grace started studying the US trade magazines. Our first and most successful imports were *Chick-*

enman, Dr Joyce Brothers, Our Changing World, and *The Passing Parade*.

Grace herself was responsible for obtaining these shows. She discovered *Chickenman* when it was mentioned in *Time* magazine, Dr Joyce came from NBC, and the other two were found in a trade magazine.

Dr Joyce Brothers and *Our Changing World* became important programme additives on stations across Australia, New Zealand, and other Gibson markets. Dr Brothers was a psychologist who talked mainly about sexual matters and women's topics generally. She was popular and the programme drew a great deal of mail. All the letters we received were sent to Dr Brothers for a reply. The feature ran for 2,600 episodes in Australia alone!

We released 3,000 episodes of *Our Changing World*. The host was Earl Nightingale, who had a wonderfully deep voice and an engaging manner. He simply talked about a better way of life. He was a great motivator and many of his ideas are still stored in my memory.

Grace was very excited about *Chickenman*, a spoof of super heroes like Superman. Quick off the mark she contacted the producer and asked about the possibility of selling his show in our markets. Being a small company, they agreed and sent over 195 episodes. Grace was so thrilled by the show she decided to audition it to our prime Sydney station 2UE herself. To her dismay, the audition was a humiliating disaster. The Feathered Fighter was rejected out of hand and it was the last time Grace approached a station in person with a new show.

The initial sale we made was to 5AD Adelaide. Then I took it to Melbourne to try our luck there. We still had Ron Haig-Muir representing us and he set up my first meeting with Les Heil at 3KZ. Over lunch, Les would only offer $5 an episode. There was no way I was going to accept that, especially when no other Melbourne station had heard it. Next I went to Curteis Crawford at 3DB. He was willing to pay $7.50 an episode, but wanted the right to play it more than once. I had no worries with this; naively, I assumed he meant one repeat broadcast on the same day. Curteis had a sponsor in mind and quickly signed him up. And the deal, wait for it, was *eight* broadcasts of the same episode on the same day! What could I do? After all, the golden rule is that the man with the gold (Curteis) makes the rules.

Other capital city markets snapped up the show. The *Chickenman* phenomenon caused 2UE to have a change of heart. However, when they broadcast the White Winged Warrior in an evening timeslot — *8.30 pm!* — it failed. It was completely the *wrong* timeslot. I believe it was played then because the station manager did not believe in the show or understand its appeal, and wanted to sabotage it. Then came more bad news! Reaction in South Africa was completely negative; in London, even worse — the BBC almost died of shock. *Chickenman* made a slightly better landing in the Caribbean.

When I auditioned the show in New Zealand, I had great hopes. Three people sat in the room. The man in charge, Cyril, had to leave for a short time and I found myself playing one episode after another to a stony-faced middle-aged man and a middle-aged woman. *Chickenman* did not raise a laugh, let alone a smile. Not even a twitch of their lips! I was sitting there thinking, "Cyril, Cyril, come back quick or I'm dead!" Suddenly, at episode 6, the door flew open and Cyril returned. He did not even sit down. He just started to listen. And then he started to laugh. And when he laughed, the other two laughed. The sale was made. The Feathered Fighter was a fantastic success on air. But if Cyril had not come back when he did, *Chickenman* and I would both have been dead ducks!

Meanwhile back in Sydney, Ray Bean, 2UW's programme director, decided to broadcast the White Winged Warrior in the breakfast session. It was an immediate success, and now more than 50 years after it was first introduced, *Chickenman* retains its popularity.

Dick Orkin, a delightful person whom I met in Chicago, created the show. He took me walking in the notorious South Side, where I would have preferred Superman as my companion. We asked Dick to record another 65 episodes of *Chickenman* in addition to the first 195, because we wanted 260 episodes to make up a 12-month contract. Sadly, they were not of the same quality as the originals, but they sold well. Dick's other creations never achieved the same popularity. His second show, *Amazon Ace*, using the same cast as *Chickenman*, was relatively funny but was not a real hit here. *The Tooth Fairy* was next; the same cast again, but the laughs were thinner on the ground. I had to play 30 episodes to find five that were good enough to audition to 2UW. Even a later series of *Chickenman* was dreadful and was withdrawn from sale. We later learned that *The Tooth Fairy* outsold *Chickenman* in the States; perhaps they have a different sense of humour over there, or perhaps it is just their fixation with teeth.

Without doubt, our most successful featurette was *The Passing Parade*, based on John Nesbitt's famous series telling little known true stories. American John Doremus, who offered us the show, narrated it. After hearing sample episodes Grace said "Yes", and had him send the 130 episodes he had recorded. The timing could not have been better. I knew that Burns Philp, the Sydney sponsor of *Our Changing World*, wanted another featurette for broadcast on 2GB so around I went to see the station manager Percy Campbell. He was impressed by the sample he heard and said they would buy it if they could sell it to someone. I gave him the client contact details immediately, and we were on our way. 2GB purchased 260 episodes and it was scheduled immediately before the 6 pm news bulletin, a great timeslot. However, disaster struck!

Our request to John Doremus for the *next* 130 episodes brought back the bad news — *The Passing Parade* had failed in America and there would not be any more episodes. Apart from our big Sydney sale, we were picking up orders for the series everywhere. Grace was not going to let it stop. "We'll write the stories here," she said, and sent for — you guessed it — Ross Napier! She also decided we would use an Australian voice as the storyteller. But when we approached the sponsor and 2GB, both said "No" to a change of voice. They felt the show would not be a success without John Doremus's warm gravitas. So we contacted him and he was happy to voice Ross's new scripts. The scripts were written and sent to him, he recorded them and airmailed the tapes back to us. Consequently we were able to continue selling *The Passing Parade* in Australia, New Zealand, South Africa, Fiji, and the West Indies. In all, 1,500 episodes of the series were produced — 1,350 locally written. To this day I cannot understand how such a popular show failed in America.

Chicago Radio Syndicate offered us their shows. We sold *The Little People* once — to 3AW Melbourne. The problem was you could not understand the kids' voices.

MY VISIT to South Africa in 1968 brought forth some first-class one-hour plays, a locally produced version of *Address Unknown*, and a daytime serial *The Heart of Juliet Jones*. They also had a local version of *Night Beat*, but we thought it would have been sacrilege to market it. I felt that some of the South African serials fell down badly; not every episode ended with a compelling, cliffhanger climax. And some of their shows did not sell well here because their pace was too slow.

From Scotland we obtained *Mary Queen of Scots*, a great BBC serial running 130 episodes. We sold it to the ABC, but Actors Equity stopped them broadcasting it. The BBC also had a version of *The Life of Deacon Brodie*, only there was a problem — the Scottish accents were so thick you could hardly understand a word being said! A similar problem occurred with a sample of a local soapie sent from a station in Trinidad; the accents and colourful language were simply beyond comprehension.

ART Thurston was a Qantas steward with an interest in radio who often brought back new 45s from the States for some of the Sydney disc jockeys. (This was in an age where the Internet did not exist!) He then became the Australian representative for an American production company, Radio Express, which produced music shows such as the American Top 40. Art marketed them to local stations with some success.

I first met Art at a radio industry convention. We arranged to have lunch and immediately became good friends. Our company was selling locally recorded music shows at the time, and thanks to Art we obtained the right to market Radio Express shows in New Zealand where he had no contacts.

Eventually we discussed going into partnership and Art went away to consider it further. The upshot of it was that we each decided the benefits to Art would not be worth the extra work and time he would have to contribute.

Soon after, Art discovered he had stomach cancer. His operation appeared successful at first and our friendly lunches continued; because Art could not eat large meals anymore, we both ordered entrée-size portions. When Keith Graham of 2WS asked Art to join his new production company, Art agreed. (Perhaps because of his health, Art was looking for some peace and security in life.)

Unfortunately, Keith and two other executives were killed in a road accident. The new directors changed Art's agreement to his detriment. Not long after that, Art's health deteriorated and it was obvious he would not be with us for long. I was about to leave on a visit to New Zealand and paid him a visit at Prince Alfred Hospital. He was content and relaxed. I asked him to "hang around" until my return. The morning I arrived back I telephoned Art's home only to be told his funeral was being held at that moment. A couple of weeks later, I went out to Art's place and helped to clear his garage.

WHEN the new ABC radio station 2JJ started broadcasting in Sydney,

I decided to listen and find out what it was all about. The breakfast session was good and heralded a brand new comedy — *Chuck Chunder of the Space Patrol*. I was so impressed that I wanted to do a deal with the producers and sell it through our company. I quickly got onto the ABC and discovered that I was going to have to deal directly with *Chuck Chunder's* creators, Tony Sattler and Garry Reilly, who owned the rights. Their company was named RS Productions; one assumes the RS stood for their names, although after I started dealing with them I believed it could have also stood for something else! I thought they were a pain in the neck but I liked them. They thought the same of me so all was fair. In fact Tony once called me a right wing Liberal-voting Catholic bastard, to which I replied, "I'm a Protestant, not a Catholic." I repaid him later by telling him that his girlfriend looked like an old bag and was old enough to be his mother. He took that well. She even sent me her autographed photograph! When it was Grace's turn to meet Tony and Garry, she was shocked. I do not think she thought they were a breath of fresh air, though she had to admit they were different from her usual associates. Despite all the aggravation, the negotiations were positive. (Fortunately I did not have to deal with all the ABC's legal processes.) We got the rights to market *Chuck Chunder*, although Tony screwed me down to a 40% share of the sales revenue instead of the 50% I wanted. At last we were on our way with a brand new comedy, something lacking in our library. New Zealand thought it was good and they sold it nationally, and we made some profitable commercial sales in Australia as a bonus. Meanwhile, Tony and Garry went on to create those famous comedies *The Naked Vicar Show* and *Kingswood Country*.

Today, as I write this, 2JJ is celebrating its thirtieth birthday. I wonder where all those creative young people who created the station are now?

Episode 11

The Napier Line

ROSS Napier had just left school when he sold his first script. It was 1949, he was only 17, and he had written an episode for one of 2GB's most famous shows, *Doctor Mac*.

Like Reg Johnston, Ross's contribution to Grace Gibson Radio Productions was incalculable. Every aspect of radio drama called to him: beyond the writing, he was enthralled by the arts of direction and crafting a sound. He wrote our greatest book adaptations such as *Cattleman*, and pioneered the shorter-length serials; he wrote so much for us that his DNA became part of ours. Apart from me, Ross had a longer association with Grace Gibson than anybody else.

He was also my best friend for many years. And although *The Castlereagh Line* was our greatest combined success, it was also the cause of our friendship's demise. Our friendship's end was brutal and irreconcilable.

ROSS and I shared a passionate love of radio. And, like me, he started out as an office boy, working for one of Grace's competitors, Associated Programmes-Towers of London. I first got to know him when we collected pressings from the Australian Record Company with all the other office boys. It was there that Ross read us — very dramatically — the first love scene he had ever written for a radio serial. We thought it was so dreadful that we all fell about laughing. Ross had the last laugh; his second acceptance was a half-hour script for 2UE's *Authors' Playhouse*. Next, he went to see Grace. She suggested he write a script for *Night Beat*. When Reg Johnston read it, he bought it on the spot. It became episode 19!

When Michael Plant announced his decision to go to London, a replacement was needed. Grace offered Ross a staff position — writing and editing scripts, and doing sound effects. He jumped at it. He joined the staff in 1951, and continued writing for the company until 1986. His first day at work was the day of Reg Johnston's funeral.

Ross's first assignment was *Alias the Baron*. He had to turn Anthony Morton's best-selling novel of the time, *Meet the Baron*, into 104 15-minute episodes. To complicate the task, the central character in the book always worked alone — not a great starting point because radio was all about dialogue! Ross told me it was a dreadful creative experience.

At first, Grace and Ross worked closely. She discussed his scripts in detail, especially the first few episodes of a show. Ross wrote a week or two ahead of recording deadlines, and while tapping out 1,300 episodes of *Portia Faces Life* was a herculean task, his greatest challenge was the soapie *The Guiding Light*, based on American scripts. He told Grace how bad they were, only to be told, "But, Ross, they're *American* scripts!" She believed there was nothing much to do, just change a few words, but in the end Ross completely rewrote each episode. Even in those early days, Ross was not given to compromise.

To my mind, Ross's skills were innate. He was a born radio writer. He had no formal training as a writer or doing sound effects; he simply developed his skills by trial and error. Unlike most writers in radio, Ross had a lot of contact with the casts. He was often in the studio doing sound effects; he loved creating the creeping footsteps coming down the stairs, and the fist fights. Those early days helped shape Ross as a writer.

He sometimes wrote with specific actors in mind, tailoring scripts to their range, to what they could do well. Alan White was always Ross's favourite Randy Stone. According to Ross, no one was better at first-person narration. White was great to write for.

SHORTLY after Ross joined the staff and we had become friends, we decided we would go on holidays together. We thought it would be fun to take a sea trip from Sydney to Perth. Ross had his holiday approved, so I went in to see Grace and apply for my leave too.

She was most upset. Letting me take leave was not the issue; she did *not* want her two juniors going off on an ocean adventure together. Perhaps she thought it would breed insubordination on our return. We pleaded with her but her answer was a stony "No".

In the end she solved the problem. She refused to give me my holidays.

IN LATER years, Ross developed an obsession with money. It became unpleasant and destructive, but its genesis was clear. He started at £13 a week. And while that was three times the weekly wage that other young men his age received, most freelance radio writers were paid £4 *a script*. Not surprisingly, he eventually went in and asked Grace for a pay rise. According to his calculations, he should have been earning £28 a week. Grace refused. Instead, she explained how she was subsidising his being there and learning his craft.

After four years, with no decent pay rise in sight, Ross resigned. I hated to see him leave, but I did not blame him. He had married Ann Fuller, one of Grace's script typists, and had established himself as one of Australia's leading radio drama writers. He was serious about radio; now it was time to earn some serious money. Grace was furious. She behaved as though he had betrayed her.

Ross took a scriptwriting job with Creswick Jenkinson at Associated Programmes-Towers of London, replacing Peter Yeldham who was going to England. He wrote *Address Unknown* and *Smoky Dawson* for £40 a week. *Address Unknown* was one of Australia's best-loved drama series. Originally created by Jenkinson, it featured documentary-dramas taken "from the files of the Missing Persons Bureau". Ross took over from Peter for another 200 episodes, many of which he continued to write when he, too, went to England in 1956.

ROSS wrote more scripts for Grace than anybody else and had less trouble. He knew exactly what Grace wanted. Sometimes he would go a bit too far and Grace would drawl, "Ross …"

Ross wrote the bulk of Grace's serials from the 1960s onwards, and he would have been the only writer to sustain a career throughout those years. His radio-writing credits are endless. He was equally at home scripting half hour and quarter hour self-contained daytime series, 15-minute serials, and book adaptations. It was Ross who created the demanding 4- and 6-minute serials that radio wanted from the 1970s onwards.

Ross had two great qualities — discipline and dedication. He worked out a writing schedule and stuck to it. Some writers were always late handing in scripts. Some were even known to be writing on the bus coming to the studio, or finishing a script during a lunch break. It did not help the quality of their work. Significantly, Ross provided shorter story synopses than other writers who complicated their stories with pages of details. By doing so they proved they could not write well. Ross would seldom submit more than half a page — it was all he needed to sell his ideas. Ross also had the ability to come up with the great titles and imaginative openings we prized so much. Was he Grace Gibson's best writer? I believe Grace shared my opinion that he was.

By the demise of radio drama, Ross was being paid more than any other Gibson writer. "Kath Carroll would have died if she'd have known," he admitted once.

ROSS and Ann headed for London in 1956. Ross said later, "I left a couple of the best years of radio behind. I went to England to get TV experience. We all had a feeling that TV was coming, but I didn't think it was going to do what it did. It wiped out radio serials virtually overnight. Suddenly it was all over. The actors were talking about it in the studio — television's coming to gobble us all up."

When Ross returned to Sydney, he started writing *Skippy* and *Number 96*; radio became a second interest. He did not write for us for a while as he did not have time. He had a falling out with the *Number 96* people over money. And he would not write for Crawfords because they would not pay him enough money. I am not knocking having money, but Ross seemed to get more and more obsessed with it. Radio never paid all that well, but we all did okay out of it. Perhaps, after all those years of scrimping and arguing with Grace about his fees, Ross had developed an unhealthy demand for higher and higher rates of pay. In fact, I am sure that was the cause of his later behaviour.

ROSS pioneered our shorter-length dramas, but his best was yet to come in 1982. *The Castlereagh Line* was one of the most popular Grace Gibson shows of all. It ran for 910 six-minute episodes and was broadcast in every radio market in Australia, and most of the company's overseas markets.

We had read Don Whitington's book *King Hit*. Ross saw its potential, and bought the radio rights himself. He not only wrote the serial, but also fulfilled a lifelong ambition by directing it. However, there was one monumental difference: Ross did not want a script fee — he wanted a share of the gross. Grace had been paying him about $10 an episode for writing the 6-minute serials. She paid him more than anybody else. But for *The Castlereagh Line*, Ross agreed to 25% of the gross in lieu of script fees. Fair enough. He owned the rights, and he was going to direct the production as well. He would be working a lot harder. I thought the matter was settled; 25% to Ross, 75% left to cover cast and production costs, and our profit margin. But I was wrong.

Having agreed to 25% of gross earnings, Ross suddenly wanted a higher cut. Literally within the course of a lunch with our company manager Ralph Taylor, Ross had secured an increase commencing after the initial 130 episodes. I lost my appetite.

Ross poured himself into the project. Firstly, he researched the locations where the story was set. He drove to the old coaching stations around Tamworth and Glen Innes, soaking up the history and atmosphere. Then, in a big departure from the traditional practice of using library music in radio dramas, he decided the show should have its own unique theme music — a specially recorded song, like movies and TV shows have. He wrote his lyrics to the tune of *Lilly Bolero* (also known as *Lillibullero*, an Irish melody used by the BBC World Service as its signature theme). The evocative song would open each episode together with the authentic sound of a Cobb & Co coach.

He also wanted the show produced in the style of a film production, recording scenes out of sequence. And to achieve a more contemporary stereo sound — something more in the realm of a Dolby movie soundtrack — the show was recorded and digitally mixed at the Madrigal studio in North Sydney.

Not only did audiences overwhelmingly respond to the show, the actors did too. The new breed of actors did not look down on radio; they wanted to do it. When we were casting *The Castlereagh Line*, we were told that we would never get the people we wanted for the money we were going to pay. But we worked out ways, because they all wanted to come in and do it. It was good training for them too. People like Belinda Giblin were big stars in television, but she loved recording *The Castlereagh Line*. Her radio acting improved once she started working with people like Ric Hutton, who was a past master of the art of radio acting. I remember one scene where Ric had a pencil in his mouth when he was talking, because he was meant to be eating, and all these young actors were looking at him unbelievably. Fancy putting a pencil in your mouth!

At a time when radio drama had long been unfashionable, it took a brave programmer to start the ball rolling in Sydney. Ray Bean, who had seen the potential of *Chickenman* at 2UW, was now programme director of 2WS. Bean bought *The Castlereagh Line* for the new Western Sydney station. As he explained, "The philosophy of the station then was very much to support Australian content. Our programming objective was to play contemporary Australian music, at a time when Australian music was still having a battle getting content to air." The same philosophy embraced drama. The station wanted local drama in its lineup; the problem was finding the correct product. "We could see that the right material would work very well. In the old days of drama it was the 15-minute session, but of course radio had moved to a tighter format. The old serials faded out because people didn't have time to sit down and listen to them. *Dr Paul* and *Portia Faces Life* and all those things were very old in their style and content, they'd had their day." Instead, Bean was keen to experiment with short dramas. His judgement proved correct.

The Castlereagh Line was playing on over 60 stations around Australia and overseas. Even a little station on the Isle of Man played it, as did Zimbabwe Broadcasting to great success judging by all the African fan mail. We almost had a sale in the United States, although they finally turned it down because our language was a tad too rough for the poor Americans. They do not know what they missed!

I believe that one of the key selling points for the show had been our guarantee of a logical conclusion every 65 episodes. Very few stations stopped before episode 910, and most wanted the story to continue, but Ross called a halt.

ROSS had been my best friend for many years. But the rot set in when we were in production for the final series of *The Castlereagh Line*. He came to me with what I thought was an unreasonable increase in fee. I was shocked; it was an outrageous money grab, basically blackmail. I refused to agree but left the decision to our general manager, Brian Byrne at Alberts. I told Brian, "If you're going to give it to him — okay, but I'm not going to." Brian worked out a compromise because of the difficult position in which we were placed.

Our production arrangement was that Ross would provide scripts for each of the 65 episodes at the one time, so that recording of voice tracks could be completed in one week. This made it better for the casts as far as money was concerned, and also kept them for a minimum of time. They were very happy with the arrangement, although some of them pointed out that they would not normally work for such small fees. In fact, they were all very keen to be involved in radio drama; it was an opportunity to work with more experienced actors and for some to learn a new craft. The music and sound effects were added later, but it was a long process and an expensive one.

The argument over increased fees produced bitter consequences. During the final series of *The Castlereagh Line*, Ross did not stick to the deal. He sent in the scripts in dribs and drabs. The schedule was delayed, the cast was unhappy, and costs increased. Not that it mattered to Ross; he did not share the costs, he just wrote and directed. Some of the actors were complaining about the unnecessary delays and the general waste of everyone's time that Ross was causing. I tried to reason with him, to mollify him. I remember telling him that his daughter Linzi would make a lot of money out of *The Castlereagh Line* because it would still be playing when he was dead and gone. I was trying to convince him to take a longer view of his income and not expect everything at once. It went down like a lead balloon.

Our relationship deteriorated further.

We had encouraged Ross to write novels based on the radio series, and had co-operated in their marketing by promoting them to stations. We allowed his wife Ann to use our facilities for packing and despatch of the books. We provided the means for Ross and Ann to attend the annual broadcasting convention where they could meet station managers and work hard to get extra sales. We were paid a small commission for the sale of each book. When Ross increased the price of the books, we requested a small increase in our share of the profits. It was denied.

THE CASTLEREAGH LINE was the first major Gibson show to be digitally produced. Ross was aspiring for excellence, but without realising it, we had entered treacherous waters. From time to time I believed there was something "wrong" with the sound quality. It seemed to happen from episode 100 on. Ross and I were horrified to hear sound effects occasionally change perspective on air. A cow supposedly mooing in a field sounded more like it was in bed with the heroine. Hisses and sibilance dogged the dialogue. Worse, the effects seemed to change from station to station. Instead of stereo sound, sometimes the show only came through one speaker. In fact, one New Zealand station stopped the series because it was fed up with the sound quality.

Ross and I thought about it continually but John Woodward, who was technical director, assured us everything was okay. A little while later, a technician from Melbourne contacted me and said there was a basic fault with the recordings — some episodes had been recorded "out of phase". That did not mean much to me, but investigations proved him right. Without being too technical, either the two studio microphones or the stereo analogue recorder had been set up incorrectly, creating an "out of phase" situation. Apparently, phasing often occurs when two microphones are used that are not identical, or when cables connected to the microphones do not match, or when the stereo recorder needs to be serviced. Any engineer worth his salt would be alert to this. It was a disaster waiting to happen. Phasing resulted when two identical signals are inverted; when played back in mono, they cancel each other out! Carelessness at the recording studio was to blame. It was too late to seek compensation from the recording company; Madrigal had gone out of business.

Even though it was a recording company's mistake, I considered that both John Woodward and Ross were at fault. John, being technical director, should have been aware that there was a problem. And Ross was overall director of the show; I felt that he should have been more diligent and pinpointed the problem earlier. About 300 episodes were affected. As Ross had just been given a fee increase and was responsible for the overall production, it was my opinion that he should contribute to the overall costs of rectifying the sound. He refused and said it was nothing to do with him. When I employed the Melbourne technician to fix the problems, Ross complained that the process was too slow and that our Sydney studio (owned by 2UW and Alberts) should do it. If we went down that route, I explained to him, the costs would be enormous. He was not satisfied and complained to Brian Byrne, who called a meeting to thrash out the problem. Ross brought Ann with him. Tempers were frayed between the three of us. I end up telling her to mind her own bloody business and that finished the meeting. Some weeks later I invited Ross to come into the office for a chat about how we might resolve the problem. We ended up having a beer and I thought our differences were forgotten. But they were not.

I HAVE no doubt whatsoever that *The Castlereagh Line* could have continued for a lot longer, but clearly Ross had had enough. Later on, he produced audition episodes of a serial that was related to *The Castlereagh Line*. He never offered it to us, but negotiated with other companies and sent samples of it directly to station managers. His venture failed. He demanded the same high fees that he had squeezed out of us, but other companies would not pay the price. Also, the radio stations did not want to do business directly with Ross because they did not know whether he would be able to provide the product reliably. It was a shame. If Ross had wanted to write again, I am sure we would have eventually worked out a deal.

Some years later he agreed to be interviewed for the book about Grace — *Yes, Miss Gibson*. He co-operated and gave us excellent material but still harped on about money. "She [Grace] was the greatest bitch. And that was the peculiar part about it. You spent your life cursing her, but she was a woman you respected for some reason. I didn't do badly from her, it was a fairly happy arrangement, and she did become a little more generous. But she *was* bloody tight…" The meeting was pleasant but clearly he was not interested in reviving our friendship. It was the last time I saw him alive.

When Ross died on Melbourne Cup Day, November 2004, Ann told no one of his passing. None of his friends knew what had happened to him. He had seemingly just disappeared. We thought the situation was very odd and made some enquiries. Eventually we found out from his golf club that he had indeed passed away, but even the club had not been able to find out more about the circumstances of his death. Eventually, business reasons forced Ann to admit that Ross was gone. He had suffered a massive stroke. It was a devastating moment, and I was angry. I felt *cheated*. Ross and I had shared many a drink after so many funerals, and I would have loved having one or two for him. I still consider Ross was my best friend. We had been through so much together and shared so many triumphs.

ROSS and Ann had a beautiful old house in Longueville, on a double block of land with a view down to Riverview. The house had so many rooms that Ross and Ann lived in only part of it.

They had bought it very cheaply as an investment. The last time I saw it, the old place needed a completely new roof and lots of other things done. But no matter what state it is in now, it would have to be worth in the millions.

The Castlereagh Line had been our greatest success. As two old mates, we should have been celebrating its success. Instead, it marked the end of a beautiful friendship.

Episode 12

Down But Not Out

IN 1971, Grace moved the company to smaller premises in North Sydney. Our offices and studio were now at ADC House on the Pacific Highway at North Sydney, directly opposite the railway station. Our numbers were down to just Grace, her assistant Noreen Tweeddale, John Woodward and me, and a receptionist. John was directing, operating the panel, cutting masters, maintaining equipment, casting, editing scripts, and doing all the cost sheets.

But the good news was after all those windowless years in Savoy House and City Mutual, we now had harbour views; one looked across the Bridge to the city, the other out to the Heads. Because the despatch area provided such a stunning view of Middle Harbour, Grace allocated me a small office at the end of a corridor. There was no way she would let me have views in both my work areas! It was so typical of Grace, and I was not too pleased. Fortunately, our disagreements rarely lasted. Eventually she relented and allowed me to use her office when entertaining clients and whenever she was not there.

It was around this time that Grace used to enjoy rewriting her Will. She sat in her office contemplating her decisions. If I went in to ask her something, she always looked at me sternly and said that I "wasn't in it". All I could do was smile. Occasionally, Noreen and I would be asked to witness her signature.

By the mid-1970s, at least sixty per cent of Grace's revenue came from overseas sales. In fact, in most English-speaking broadcasting markets, Grace Gibson was the BBC Transcription Service's sole competitor. She enjoyed nothing more than being a bean counter. Every so often she would call me in and ask, "Tell me, Reg, how much have we got back on *Dossier on Dumetrius*?"

SOMETIMES, even in the 1970s, writers found us.

Russ Writer (yes, the surname *is* correct!) was one of the last of the old-school scriptwriters. He came to see me and shared a very sad story. When he was told to finish up at 2GB as a salaried employee, he went in to see Des Foster the manager. Des asked him what he did. Russ was devastated. Over the years, he had written some of their top-rating serials such as *Superman* and dozens of others. He was one of their main scriptwriter-directors in the golden age of radio, but Des did not have a clue! Now he was on the scrap heap. (He would have been shocked to learn what Ross Napier was earning from us!) I felt quite sorry for Russ so we decided to assign him one of our new shorter-length dramas, *River of Destiny*, based on *The Pathway of the Sun* by E. V. Timms. Kath Carroll had originally adapted the book many years before as a 52 episode 15-minute serial. Kath had done a brilliant job, the show had sold well, so we had renewed the rights and now wanted Russ to script the same book as a 130 episode 6-minute serial. (However, we could not give him Kath's scripts to go on.)

Apparently, Russ got into trouble around episode 30. Unbeknownst to us, he delved into another story by the same author — *Forever to Remain* — and started lifting great chunks from it! Unfortunately for us, Mr Timms's son was living in Nowra and listening to the show. When he realised that one of his father's other books had been "hijacked", he reported it to the publisher. When I took the call, I knew we were in serious trouble. Literary larceny is not treated lightly. Russ had dropped us into the proverbial. I was furious. If only I had known what Russ was doing I could have jumped on it. We had to cease and desist playing the serial and pay compensation. Thankfully, we got out of it pretty well without going to court.

Russ was working on another serial for us — *Time is the Catcher*. He drove me berserk with that show too. There was no plot and very poor characters. Russ's biggest problem was that he was deadline pusher; he would always be writing scripts on the bus on the way to the studio, pushing things out at the last minute. Perhaps it was because he had always been on salary at 2GB and never had to work independently, competing in the open market like Ross Napier. He also had a variety of health issues that slowed him down. Russ was a lovely chap, one of the legends, but terribly unreliable.

In the early 1970s, after we relocated to ADC House in North Sydney, an envelope of scripts were slipped under our door one morning. They were the first two episodes and synopsis of *Under Her Spell*, written by Jim Aitchison who worked for an advertising agency, Paton Australia, a few floors below us. Grace snapped them up at once, telling Jim that John Saul would have loved his writing. I wonder whether Jim would have ever fulfilled his ambition to write radio serials if we had not been in the same building?

Then, in the early 1980s, author Judy Nunn approached us with a concept for a show inspired by the Azaria Chamberlain case. Neryl likes Judy's books, and I had read one or two which I liked, so I was keen to see her scripts. As soon as I read them I was horrified to discover that the central character was going to be the baby Jesus — and the dingo was going to steal Him! I had to tell Judy that it would not be acceptable to muck around with Jesus like that — particularly with a surname like Nunn!

COME 1978, Grace Gibson Radio Productions was in its thirty-fourth year. Grace had produced 200 different shows; 37 had used American scripts, the rest had been written by Australians. Hundreds of her old transcriptions, once the pride and joy of my huge despatch department, had been despatched to the National Film and Sound Archive of Australia in Canberra. Many more were still playing, somewhere in the world. It was also the year when Grace and Ronnie made their final visit to the States where she spent a number of weeks in hospital recovering from an "overdose of drugs".

It was clear to me that both she and Ronnie were in failing health. Grace was taking dangerous cocktails of drugs to combat a variety of ailments, real or imagined. Her system was paying the price. Her problem was that she went to so many different doctors, they all gave her tablets to take, but she did not tell them that she had received medication from other doctors. She said she had a bad heart, but her doctor here, a top man, said she did not. A doctor in Honolulu confirmed the diagnosis. Grace did not believe either of them. She had had a number of operations for cancer too, always when she was in the United States. Not for a moment did I believe she had cancer; nor did I see the necessity for yet another operation. When Grace returned to Sydney, I could see she was ready to give it all away. She was just tired and worn out. She was 73; she had had a tough life, now it was time to stop. But first she had to find a way out of the company that bore her name. It was obvious that she did not know what to do. She was concerned about the staff — about her assistant Noreen, John Woodward, and me.

Keith Graham was about to open 2WS, the first new AM radio licence granted in Sydney in 46 years. Keith and one of his directors talked to me about buying Grace's company, but their workload was too great at that stage, and the talks ended.

Then an American radio producer, Harry O'Connor, wanted to buy the company and started negotiations. At the time, Grace's brother Calvin was visiting Sydney with his wife, and they were keen for her to sell as well. They talked to me and asked if I would be prepared to stay with the company after it was sold. I was the only person who knew all the programmes, and the selling and marketing of them. They said nobody would buy the company without me going along with it. I had met Harry in Los Angeles, but was unsure whether I wanted to be involved. Grace and her accountant spent time asking me to accept the change. I finally agreed to stay on, documents were prepared, everything was set, and the deal was done. Then the problems began. Harry made demands for all sorts of guarantees and no money was forthcoming. Frankly, I thought he was putting pressure on Grace to get the company without paying a dollar. I went to lunch with a very worried Grace and agreed to cable Harry saying, "Send money immediately or the deal is off". His simple reply was, "Terminate James", and the deal *was* off! He had not been a sincere buyer from the start, and that only brought more stress for Grace.

The uncertainty persisted through most of 1978. Grace was keen for her three old staffers to buy the business on very good terms. She worked out a buy-out deal for Noreen, John, and I to take over the company. I am sure it would have been an attractive deal, but I would not agree. While I could have worked with Noreen, a partnership with John Woodward would not have been possible.

Then, in early August, Nick Erby, the general manager of 2CC Canberra, called me. 2CC was the newly-licensed second commercial radio station in Canberra, owned by Capital City Broadcasters. Nick was a radio drama believer, he knew our product well, and had been 2UE's programme director when the mini-dramas first went to air. He wanted to know whether I thought Grace would sell to his company. I kept him on the phone and raced into Grace and asked her, "Would you sell?" She said, "Yes, I'd like to," so I ran back and told Nick, "Yes, she'll talk."

Two days later, Nick introduced me to the board in Canberra. They agreed to buy the business on the spot, subject to price. The directors came up to meet with Grace and settled the deal a couple of weeks later. Grace was happy; she was very comfortable with selling to Australians who shared her passion for radio drama.

By the end of August, Grace had retired. Ronnie was delighted. At last they could spend more time together. However, retirement brought some unexpected surprises for Grace. For one thing, she was shocked when Sir Edwin Hicks, the chairman of Capital City Broadcasters, gave her back her car; it had never occurred to her that her Mercedes-Benz, one of her company's assets, was part of the sale. The cost of living was another surprise. The company had covered all her living expenses for years, even her phone bills and her petrol. Now she had to do her own shopping and balance her budget, just like all those other housewives who had listened to her serials over the years!

Of course, being owned by a radio station was a real bonus for me. Overnight I was able to penetrate the inner sanctum of the broadcasting industry. I could attend the annual closed-door convention of the Federation of Australian Radio Broadcasters. Instead of having to drive from one country station to another, I had a hotel suite in which I entertained delegates and played them shows.

RONNIE died in 1981. His decline had been rapid. It were as though an athletic lifetime had left him exhausted. Grace visited him every day in St Luke's Private Hospital; I was also a regular visitor, after which I had to report to Grace on Ronnie's condition. Neryl and I often picked up Grace and Ronnie and drove them to Centennial Park where we could all chat in the open air. Grace grew very fond of Neryl during that time. She even asked Neryl to sell her beloved Mercedes-Benz; the first person who saw it, bought it. Grace did not want too much for the car, she just wanted it to go to a good home.

The day Ronnie died, I knew that Grace did not want to go on without him. Grace told an interviewer at the time, "I had the most wonderful husband, you couldn't find a more devoted husband. I've had a lot of sickness unfortunately in the last six or seven years, and he'd been by my side the whole time. I wouldn't be here if it weren't for him." I asked her for something of Ronnie's as a keepsake and she gave me his watch. Then, every time she saw me, she would put her hand on my wrist and hold on to the watch. Those moments were very special.

Ronnie's funeral service was held at St Stephen's in Macquarie Street. The staff and society friends attended. Grace asked Ross Napier and me if we would go to the Northern Suburbs crematorium with Ronnie. Noreen Tweeddale took Grace back to the penthouse.

Grace loved her penthouse, her home for a quarter of a century. Once a week, Noreen Tweeddale dropped in to do the accounts. In those final years, Grace could look back on a very full life, as she once told the press: "I'm very happy with the life that's gone before me. I did as much as I could in the time. We certainly became the leading producer of dramatic radio shows in Australia, and the world as far as that goes. There's no company that I've ever heard of that produced 66 quarter-hours a week, so I'm very happy about the past. I've had a very good life and I'm proud of the organisation that I built up and proud of the shows that we produced."

I shared her sentiments. I had devoted my working life to Grace's company, and had no regrets about staying the course when drama declined.

WITHOUT warning in late 1983, Capital City Broadcasters sold us to the Alberts family. In hindsight I should have seen it coming. Nick Erby, my ally at Capital City Broadcasters, had left. His replacement had proved uninspiring. I had so hoped that 2WS would buy us; Keith Graham and Ray Bean were stalwart supporters and offered the leadership the company needed.

On the other hand, I could see the logic of the Alberts' empire buying us. The Alberts owned 2UW Sydney, 4BC Brisbane, and a number of Queensland country stations; a famous cutting edge music studio; and the iconic Boomerang music publishing company. I was involved in the celebrations in Canberra, which enabled me to get to know all the Alberts executives better. Grace believed it would be a very positive relationship, but later events proved her wrong. On Christmas Eve 1984 — our fortieth year in the business — we vacated North Sydney and moved into Alberts' premises in Rangers Road, Neutral Bay. We were provided with new offices and a small recording studio. I was the sole surviving member of the old company. John Woodward had resigned to pursue his own freelance productions. Noreen Tweeddale, reluctant to move, had also resigned.

By then, of course, 2UW was a music station and it was hoped it could provide Gibson's with programmes that could be sold to Australian stations. Alberts also had a national representation company that would be tasked with bringing our shows to the notice of the stations they represented as well as to advertising agencies. This never happened.

Although 2UW had a very experienced staff and a happy atmosphere, it had not been very successful for some time. It was the only station that decided to transmit in AM stereo, when the rest went to FM. It had an American consultant who was thought to be a "guru" at that time; however, it seemed that Australian needs were different. Despite the fact the station was efficient, it seemed to lack proper control and this may have been the fault of the owners.

WHEN we got involved with music stations — both 2UW and 2CC — we had problems with programmes. The recording teams at those stations believed that they could just close shop for three weeks when Christmas came along. At first they did not seem to realise that when we sold a weekly music programme, the contract called for *52 broadcasts a year!* No way were we going to lose three weeks' worth of that.

It meant they had to write and produce their shows ahead of the broadcast schedule, just as we had always done in radio drama. They obviously could not do a weekly countdown, but they could do the top songs of the year, or feature particular artists. They were not terribly impressed at first but it was what *had* to be done. Music stations were not used to working this way but they got used to it.

Another venture at 2UW was commencing an overnight satellite service that transmitted a "midnight-to-dawn" programme to country stations. A price schedule had been worked out, but it was too expensive. We finally convinced 2UW to establish an overnight package similar to the rival 2UE service. However, the host of the show was not really satisfactory, and the programme offered only the 2UW music format. My belief was that it should have provided extra entertainment tailored to the needs of the stations involved.

IN 1987, someone at Alberts had the bright idea of merging Gibson's with their national representation company, and changing the name to the Radio Shop. A small committee had a weekend at Bowral to cement the plan. We were not involved until later. Numerous meetings were held and it was decided to announce the new name at the 1987 radio convention in Hobart. It was a very expensive exercise with beach bags and black sweaters being given to the delegates.

When Grace heard about it, she was bitterly disappointed. After four decades, her name had been taken off the company altogether.

By the early 1990s, the Alberts would start divesting themselves of their media interests, and our future was again in limbo.

Episode 13

Unsung Heroes

WHILE I am proud of our standards, I am the first to admit that our company did not operate in a vacuum. We enjoyed the support of some wonderful broadcasting executives. Without them, I doubt whether we would have seen our seventieth anniversary!

COUNTRY station managers were the real unsung heroes of the radio industry. They were underpaid, overworked, but stayed because of their love of the industry.

The country station managers had to know every aspect of running a station. Because they had started as junior announcers, they had the opportunity to work through all departments. All they needed was initiative and the wish to learn. They had to lead a team and know the ins and outs of everybody's job. Managers usually came from programming or sales backgrounds. From our point of view, we preferred the manager to have a programming background as it made him more concerned with the listeners' needs.

Probably my favourite station manager was **George Arklay**, who purchased programmes from us when he was at Mackay, Gunnedah, Armidale, and Taree. His general manager was fond of saying "George will buy anything"; however he never tried to interfere because George always made money for the station by buying astutely and maintaining a very happy audience.

Because of my friendship with George and the other managers of the New England Network (Tamworth-Armidale-Taree-Gunnedah-Toowoomba), we had a dinner at every radio industry annual convention. We all took it in turns to pay. I remember at the Perth convention in 1983, it was George's turn to host the group. (He was then manager of 2RE Taree.) We went to the Sheraton Hotel restaurant that was high class. Unbeknownst to George, his network colleagues had decided to really "fix" him, and selected the menu by price not by item. We started with champagne cocktails. Neryl was with us, and she fell asleep before the meal arrived! At the end of the night, when George received the account for the meal, I think he went white — but it *was* a lovely dinner.

And here I must pay tribute to **Don Thomas**, a dedicated young broadcaster. George Arklay was his mentor. I met Don at 2MO Gunnedah shortly after he became manager; George was sitting in the manager's chair with Don sitting opposite. Don was only in his early twenties, very creative, full of ideas. While George would never have wanted to move to a capital city station, I am sure that Don would have been a success if he had made the move.

Don is constantly in touch with me, keeping me up to date with radio happenings and provides me with a lot of worthwhile material. I was delighted to assist him in the special programmes he produced for the 50th Anniversary of 2MO, and the 75th of 2AD Armidale, from where he retired.

From time to time I receive telephone calls from a number of my broadcasting friends, and I wish I could name them all. Suffice to say, I am always pleased and grateful when they call me.

MOST of the top station managers in the capital cities started in the bush and consequently knew their jobs well. My number one broadcaster was **Alan Faulkner** who came to 2UE Sydney from 2KO Newcastle.

The Lamb family owned both stations. Alan had been general manager at 2KO, and I had met him on my first country trip. The smart people started calling 2UE "the only country station in the city". How they ate their words! Alan introduced the Top 40 format, and launched a magazine format in the mornings that was the envy of all. No one else could emulate its success. 2UE quickly increased its audience and introduced the slogan "At or near the top".

Alan also purchased a lot of Grace Gibson shows over the years. On one occasion, Grace was keen for me to audition a new serial she had received, but which neither of us had heard. I think she got it from Harry Alan Towers. I took it to Alan and it was a disaster. The story was poor, and the sound on the 16-inch transcription was disgraceful. I was terribly embarrassed, but Alan was polite about it. Never again did I offer a show without first hearing it!

Alan was a serious man, well respected, generous, true to his word, and always courteous. Whenever I went to see him, he would leave his office and come to reception to greet me. Above all, he was honest and caring.

Another favourite of mine was **Bill Stephenson**. He left an executive position at 2UE to take up the challenge of turning 2SM Sydney from a religious station into a top-rating station. I knew Bill only casually, but liked what he did at 2SM. He obviously picked good staff and later became a leader of the industry. He was very successful, a serious and reliable man, and a member of the famous Stephenson clan that started 2UE way back in 1925.

I also wonder what heights that **Keith Graham**, the founding general manager of 2WS in Sydney's West, would have reached had he not died so tragically in a car accident with two of his colleagues. I think Keith started his career at 2MO Gunnedah; I first knew him when he was the manager of 7HO Hobart. Later he was the founding manager at 2GO Gosford. At that time, 2WS was just a dream of men who recognised what the west of Sydney would become.

I had always wanted Keith to buy Grace's company; under his progressive leadership our future would have been assured. It was not to be. However at one stage Keith offered me the chance to join his new production company, Seven Hills Productions. Perhaps Keith decided to start the company when he could not buy Grace Gibson Productions. Seven Hills distributed US shows, and was looking to obtain Art Thurston's programmes. It was a tempting offer but the deal was for a one-year contract with the future depending on results. It was too difficult to reach a decision so I stayed where I was.

I do not believe there would be any argument that **Lewis Bennett**, general manager of 3UZ, led the field in the Melbourne scene. 3UZ started in 1925, founded by Oliver John Nilsen, manufacturer of electric jugs, kettles, toasters, crystal wirelesses, and radios. His station was consistently at the top of the ratings for sixty years. Lewis Bennett was an icon of Melbourne radio, a shrewd broadcaster famous as an immaculate dresser with his signature bow tie. He led his station to glory under the banner "The Greater 3UZ".

Two managers for whom I had tremendous respect were **Les Heil** of 3KZ Melbourne and **Derek Low** from across the water in New Zealand. After losing management roles, they took on relatively menial positions until they had fought their way back to the top of their profession. Both revived the fortunes of ailing stations and led them to ratings leadership.

Des Foster of 2GB Sydney became an excellent Director of the Federation of Australian Commercial Broadcasters, leading the industry through difficult times. He fought many crucial battles over music copyright. The first time I met Des he was the manager of 2UE Sydney. He then moved to 2GB. Years later in 1978, when we were owned by 2CC (Capital City Broadcasters), I attended the annual broadcasters' convention over Des's objections. After it finished I told him how much I had enjoyed the experience. His stern reply was, "You shouldn't be here!" He tried to ban me from the next convention too; I think I mollified him by not attending financial or contentious sessions. In the bus returning from a Tasmanian restaurant, he and 2UW's Frank Jeffcoat insisted I sing; I took that to mean Des had finally accepted me. Des was not a drama fan and when I told him that 2CH had received more than 5,000 letters from listeners wanting *Dr Paul* and *Portia Faces Life* to continue, he would not believe me. I offered to deliver the letters to his office, but he just smiled and walked away. When I was attempting to obtain an Order of Australia for Grace, I asked Des for a letter on her behalf. He agreed to help. After the award was announced I rang to thank him, only to learn that he too had received an award.

Finally, I must include **Frank Jeffcoat** in my tributes. Ironically, Frank was the man who took drama off 2UW Sydney in 1964, much to Grace's regret. Frank succeeded in the difficult task of rebuilding the station's audience and commanded the respect of our industry.

NOW it is time to embarrass a couple of special broadcasters.

Even though **Ray Bean** was the programme manager who changed 2UW's format and stopped the morning serials, he remains one of my favourite radio people. Ray was "out there", forging ahead with new formats, challenging the sacred cows, bucking conventional industry wisdom, and above all was a straight shooter. Ray constantly defied the trends; he brought *Chickenman* to 2UW after it had failed on 2UE, and scored great success. From 2UW he was appointed general manager of the new station 3MP, on Melbourne's Mornington Peninsula, when it started transmission. Despite the fact it was a music station, Ray used short features that gave the audience exactly what it wanted. He returned to the Sydney market as programming manager of 2UE. In just one survey, he turned 2UE from a very ordinary station into the top rating one. He did not last long there because a new general manager decided that he knew more about programming than Ray did. Hence

Ray moved on to a new station in Sydney's Western Suburbs, 2WS, commencing his legendary partnership with Keith Graham.

I had lunch with Ray in 1991, just after he had a heart bypass operation. He was telling me about it and I was listening because I was about to have the same operation! He came to visit me when I was in hospital, and it was something we had in common for all those years after. I believe he is now in a nursing home and not very well.

In August 1978, **Nick Erby** of Capital City Broadcasters — owners of 2CC Canberra —headed up the negotiations to buy Grace's company. 2CC had taken Canberra by storm and captured fifty per cent of the audience. Nick was one of the new breed of broadcasters; others were Keith Graham, Ray Bean, and 4GG's Barry Ferber. I had first met Nick when he was programme manager of 2UE; at the time, it was the most successful station in Australia. He was keen on country music and asked me for a copy of 50-hour country music special we were distributing. As he was not going to broadcast or pay for it, I said "No". The first thing Nick did after becoming our general manager was to request the show again. Naturally, I obliged.

Nick had a vision for *our* future! He did not see us as a relic of the past; he believed our best years were still to come. He and I went to the United States in December 1978 in search of new shows and concepts. (That was when I observed how caring he was of his staff. We were driving along Sunset Boulevard when the vehicle behind hit us, pushing us into the limo in front. Nick's only concern was whether I was okay.) He pumped up our resources. Suddenly we had two new staff members, up-to-the-minute office machines, and for me — a car! I sometimes thought that the car was there just so I could drive him to the airport, always at the last minute. On the way he would regularly tell me I would be sacked if he missed the plane.

As part of Nick's vision was a corporate re-launch. Grace Gibson Radio Productions would become simply Gibson. I had no objection to the name change because I knew everyone would still recognise us as Grace Gibson's. The re-launch happened at the next annual conference of the Federation of Commercial Broadcasters. It was a 3-day event. More than 100 broadcasters attended. We produced a great new catalogue, we had a suite for entertaining, a price list for every station, plus food and drinks. The conference was a major success.

Nick was a passionate radio dramaphile — so much so that he conceived and wrote the first Australian radio serial set in the corridors of political power. *The Priestman File* was about a man who wanted to be Prime Minister. (Until then, no one had ever thought of making a serial involving the rough and tumble of federal politics; Nick was an original thinker.) But his passion was soon eroded by all the calls on his time and the demands of management. It was Nick's first go at writing long-form radio. Pleasure became pain, but he struggled to keep writing. *The Priestman File* was not exactly a four-minute serial, nor was it precisely a six-minute serial. Nick got sick of writing it at about episode 40. I pleaded with him, "You can't just stop. We've sold 65 episodes and I'm not going back to the stations to tell them it's only 40 episodes. You *have* to write another 25!" I reminded him it was hard enough to sell radio drama; suddenly leaving stations in the lurch would make the next sale near to impossible. Originally we had agreed that each episode would run six minutes, but Nick was determined to get to the end as quickly as possible. I think at one stage he had one episode down to about 60 seconds! He was really battling to get it finished; only a handful of writers can sustain a marathon story.

One of Nick's strong attributes was his ability to select top people who were keen to contribute. Nick was the leader we needed. When he said something had to be done, it was done. Rob Mackay and his personal assistant Maggie worked wonders. There were many others on Nick's team, all great people, but after 40 years their names elude me. Of course, Nick was not popular with everyone because he could be abrasive and was never slow to give his opinion. On one occasion I asked him who was the best manager in a particular network. He quickly responded with such-and-such a name, adding "the best of a bad bunch". It gave me a laugh. However, Nick's biggest problem, as I saw it, was frustration. He wanted to fly and take the company where the directors were not sure they wanted to go. They had their success with 2CC and were very happy. In the end, Nick resigned. From my point of view I was very disappointed. While Gibson would continue, I missed Nick's involvement, enthusiasm, and contribution.

The final idea he gave us was his best. He had discovered the novel *King Hit* from which we produced our biggest success, *The Castlereagh Line*. Nick was not there to enjoy its amazing popularity through the 1980s until today. And this was in the era when the majority of commercial broadcasters considered there was no place for radio drama. Our triumph was indeed Nick's.

Nick is now happily enjoying life in Tweed Heads. He was a good friend of the late Keith Graham; although very different in personality, together they would have been a great combination.

ONE of the most remarkable things about the radio industry was throughout its "golden days" we never had a bad debt.

When Sydney stations stopped playing drama, they owed Grace Gibson a lot of money, but there was never any doubt that they would pay. (The only exception was 3AK Melbourne, which tried to avoid paying but eventually did.) The smaller markets were just as honourable. I have never forgotten the owner of a small NSW station, 2XL Cooma. Through no fault of his, the station had terrible financial problems. It may have taken a long time but the debt was finally paid.

I SHOULD also bear testimony to the great radio announcers of the golden age. They were legendary on-air salesmen. Back in the 1940s, two of the best were gravel-voiced **John Harper** on 2KY, and **Allan Toohey** of 2UE and later 2UW.

Broadcasting over 2KY, "the Labor station" in George Street, John had his own compelling style, or lack thereof! Many present-day radio stars think of themselves as bold and revolutionary, more outlandish than their competitors. *Outlandish?* They do not know the meaning of the word. John Harper was the original shock-jock! If he did not like a record he smashed it — on air. He pioneered irreverence in advertising. He was once asked to stop announcing, "You can have the Pope in your home tonight". He was talking about the Pope washing machine. His humour raised many eyebrows and skated close to the borders of what was acceptable on radio in those conservative times. One such classic was an ad for Dickies beach towels. He adlibbed, "You'll see all the girls at Bondi lying on their Dickies … Dickies, the best surf towel you can buy." If that did not shock you, how about this? "There's six-and-a-half more inches in every King-size packet of Rothmans, and you girls know that's a lot of inches!" Allan, on the other hand, was the "Old Smoothie" with a beautiful voice and laid-back style.

In the early 1940s, 2GB gave us **Clark McKay**, a-happy-go-lucky breakfast announcer who was one of the first Grace Gibson narrators. When commercial broadcasting started in South Africa in the 1950s, he went there and became a household name.

NO ONE can deny the ability of the ever-popular **John Laws**. In the early 1970s, he resurrected *Dad and Dave* because he wanted a short feature on his morning show. A generation of young studio panel operators was trained specially to handle the national transmission of John's show.

Evergreen **Bob Rogers** hosted the top Sydney morning show in the 1960s and 1970s. It took a magazine format; included were our short serials such as *My Father's House* as well as our capsule features *Dr Joyce*

Brothers and *Our Changing World*. Bob was particularly fond of Dr Joyce.

Probably everybody's favourite announcer from the 1940s through to the 1980s was **Howard Craven**. Howard did everything — acting, narrating, producing. His first work was for George Edwards — that is how far back his career went! He compered 2UE's *Rumpus Room*; tens of thousands of teenagers must have flocked to this live show every afternoon. Howard was also "Charlie Chuckles", reading the comic strips out loud of a Sunday morning. He narrated *Night Beat* and appeared in countless shows of ours. In his later years, Howard became a successful morning personality on 2CH, and his show dominated the ratings — not bad for a man in his seventies!

These announcers represent the cream of Australia's on-air talent. I could mention many more, and do not forget that most learned their craft well away from the big city markets. More importantly, they knew their job was to sell their advertisers' products and gain the respect of their audience.

Grace Gibson Radio Productions in full swing. Grace making one of her rare studio visits to greet the cast.

Grace and Ronnie celebrating my wedding to Neryl.

All four of our children attended Pymble Public School at the same time. Glenys *(foreground)* was in kindergarten, while Adam was in 6th Class, Christine in 2nd Class, and Megan in 4th Class.

At the monkey pit, Launceston, in 1981: Megan, Christine, Glenys, yours truly, and Adam.

A proud dad nursing baby Christine in October 1967.

Neryl and I dressed up for a social function in 1994.

Peter Yeldham, a great radio writer, and now a great Australian author.

The creator of *Dossier on Dumetrius*, Lindsay Hardy, at his typewriter. Looking on *(from left)* director Lawrence H. Cecil, William Eldridge, Grace, and actors Bruce Stewart and Margo Lee.

Dame Quentin Bryce, former Governor-General,
with our daughter Megan.

(Photo courtesy of Breast Cancer Network)

Paying tribute to Australia's great pioneering radio announcers: *(left)* John Harper of 2KY, and *(right)* Allan Toohey of 2UE and 2UW. "Old gravel voice" Harper preferred broadcasting in a singlet, while Toohey was smooth and urbane.

Two of my favourite unsung heroes from country radio: *(left)* George Arklay, and *(right)* Don Thomas.

(Photos courtesy of Commercial Radio Australia and 2AD)

With Grace in 1978.

Les Heil, another Melbourne radio hero.

A young Lewis Bennett. At 3UZ, he became the doyen of Melbourne broadcasting.

Thanks to painter Judy Cassab (twice winner of the Archibald Prize), Grace is still looking over my shoulder.

Episode 14

Never Off the Air

GRACE received the Order of Australia in 1987. She had often given thought to becoming an Australian citizen, but those Texan roots were too deep. It was a step she would never take. However, I believed she deserved some official recognition from her adopted land and had hurried through the nomination. Sir Alexis Albert had written a letter in support of the award, and so had Des Foster, president of the Federation of Australian Radio Broadcasters.

When I rang Grace with the news on the Queen's Birthday weekend, she was amazed. Despite all those years in radio and all those famous shows, it were as though she had no sense of her own importance in the industry.

Grace had always been gregarious, and loved nothing more than a gathering of old friends. We celebrated her eightieth birthday at our house in Pymble. Old staff and friends surrounded her. John Saul and his actress wife Georgie Sterling were there, along with Ross and Ann Napier, the Yeldhams, and our accountant. The highlight of the day came after I proposed a toast to Grace and she got up to speak. For this, Neryl brought in our four children. They were mesmerised. It was the best speech I had ever heard her give, and I wish I had recorded it. Never again would Grace entertain us so eloquently about her life and experiences.

GRACE died on 10 July 1989. I had seen her three weeks before, and it was obvious she was failing. When Noreen Tweeddale found her dead in bed and rang me, the news was not unexpected. But what followed next left me shocked. Noreen said that Grace had left a list of six names — the only people who could attend her funeral! I was on the list along with John Woodward. But she did not want Ross Napier invited, nor did she want Neryl or John's wife Betty to attend. At first, it struck me as bizarre. Why had Grace wanted to restrict her funeral to just those six names? When the initial shock wore off, I realised why. I think she might have been afraid that *nobody* would want to come, and rather than risk that, she made that strange stipulation. I was disappointed. I had wanted her to have a bigger funeral, more in accordance with her contribution to radio. Instead it was a very quiet service at the crematorium. When I contacted the media with news of her death, they were not interested. Nor was 2GB. She had been out of the public eye for a long time. So perhaps, after all, Grace's instincts had been right.

Grace's great-nephew was living in Sydney when she died. I am convinced he had a hand in the funeral arrangements. While her staff numbers had been restricted, socialities attended freely. Another mystery awaited us. Before she died, Grace had promised some of us certain paintings from her collection. There was one I absolutely loved, by the great Swiss-born Australian artist Sali Herman. John Woodward liked one with a camellia. Her solicitor was promised another. When I finally asked her nephew what had happened to the paintings, he said she had changed her mind at the last moment. In the end, he gave me a little painting of a terrace in Woolloomooloo, which at first I hated; it's by quite a well-known artist and now I have grown to love it. But there was definitely "funny work" going on, same as with her funeral. And as for the penthouse, that went under the hammer quickly.

When Michael Plant had died back in the 1960s, Grace, Ronnie, and I had attended his funeral at the Northern Suburbs Crematorium.

On the spot they decided they would like to be cremated there, too. Grace loved all the gardens, and that is where they are. Neryl and I went out to see her plaque in a brick wall. Ronnie is next to her. I would prefer to have my ashes spread.

MEANWHILE on the home front, Neryl and I were catching up on all the time that we had missed together. As a family we travelled around Australia quite a lot. We used to go to Forster for family holidays, and I always went in to see my friends at 2RE Taree. The children did not mind; they usually had plenty of things to keep them occupied, or they came on station visits with me. Neryl came with me on some of my longer trips. I always drove — my motto being "I'd never fly over a radio station". It was great to have her along. Sometimes she would come and have dinner with the people at the station. It was always her decision.

I travelled the length and breadth of New Zealand too, where station executives were quite happy to see me, even on Sundays. Neryl and another couple joined me for a few weeks on one trip. The Kiwis did not like driving and could not understand why I did. In the old days, NZBC controlled commercial and national stations from Wellington; you could see all the people who mattered in one stop. With the advent of privately owned stations, my territory was now more complicated. I was serious about representing the company and thought nothing of driving from Invercargill to Whangarei and visiting all the stations in between. In some areas, the stations were so close to one another that I got to see a few of them in one day, even if it was just a quick hello. I was always treated well in New Zealand, and I was pleased to be in such a good industry.

Then, tragedy struck home.

Our daughter Megan was married in 1996. She and her husband David also bought their first home. Soon after, she was diagnosed with breast cancer. She was only 31. It was a terrible shock to Neryl and I, as well as to her siblings and of course her husband. She came over to break the news that she had found a lump in one breast. After numerous invasive tests she called us to tell us the results. We got in the car and went straight over to their place. No one else in our family had ever had a cancer diagnosis so we were all navigating unchartered territory. We did not really understand a lot of the initial medical terms and what they meant, but Megan spent a lot of time explaining them and reassuring us. I remember how difficult it was waiting for the continuing results to come in. We just wanted some good news. Megan had to undergo radiotherapy and chemotherapy, as well as several surgical procedures. She did amazingly well through the treatment, and worked as much as she could. I wondered whether that was really sensible but she explained that keeping busy kept her sane and stopped some of the negative thoughts. At the end of the day, she just wanted to feel normal.

Megan gave us all jobs to do — research, driving, cooking — and I know it was very helpful for her. She was also very conscious of the fact that people *wanted* to help her. Being part of her "support team" certainly made us feel like we were making a very small but important difference.

We knew that chemotherapy would reduce her chances of falling pregnant. It was a terrible blow for a young woman; however, she said that she had to get through the first things first. She needed to get well and then, if pregnancy was meant to be, it would happen. She had to sit back and watch all her friends having children, never really knowing if she would be blessed to have her own. As time went by, she recovered very well, got back to fitness, and looked after her body as soon as she had the energy. I remember it was a slow process as she was very tired, but she set goals for herself and before long was back to her old self.

Megan became very involved as a volunteer and as a NSW representative with the Breast Cancer Network Australia, whose patron was Quentin Bryce. In the late 1990s, there was really no information available about cancer for younger women and Megan wanted to change this. BCNA's mission was to make the journey easier, inform women of their options, and empower choice. In 2002, Neryl and I volunteered for a large event she helped organise at the Domain in Sydney. Megan spoke there about her experience and we were amongst so many people just like us who were supporting loved ones through a diagnosis. She went on to have two children; she still calls them her "miracle" children. Once, on Neryl's birthday, Megan gave her a card with a note inside to say she was going to be a grandmother *again*. I remember it was at a family barbecue. Everyone was crying at the news.

Our joy was short lived. In 2012, Megan was diagnosed with breast cancer again. It was devastating news. How could this happen again? There was to be radical surgery and more chemotherapy. At the same time Neryl was in hospital, so it was a very tough time for our family. I kept myself busy, popping down to the hospital to collect the washing from both Neryl and Megan, and return it later when I had finished laundering it. Megan confided to me, "I'm going to need your help," and the family galvanised into action. Truthfully though, there was not a lot any of us could do while she was having treatment. We just had to wait it out with her.

2015 sees Megan fit and well again. After a double mastectomy, she cannot get this dreadful disease again. She continues to work with BCNA and is now on the board. She has met some wonderful people through the Network, ranging from the former Governor-General Dame Quentin Bryce to the woman down the road who just needs an ear and a friendly word that all with be OK.

Nowadays, my greatest joys are Neryl and our grandchildren. There are seven of them — two girls, followed by 5 boys! Yes, the boys are boys, but I have to say they are very kind to me. They all help me in and out of the car, and always make sure I am comfortably seated in my chair.

Girls first. Alex is eldest, now 16 and learning to drive. She is a lifesaver and goes on patrol with her father. I am very proud of the fact she has two Duke of Edinburgh Awards, and is studying for her third.

Eliza Grace is 14; she enjoys soccer and sailing. She starts her Duke of Edinburgh Award activities this year and studies photography.

Their brother Callum is in two school bands, plays soccer, and is very keen on cards. I started teaching him three years ago. Now that he is 9, he enjoys poker and five hundred.

Next we have our eldest daughter's sons. At 11, Griffin excels at swimming, athletics, and AFL. He is also a keen inventor.

His brother Dylan is 9. Once the quietest, he is now probably the rowdiest. When he was in first class, he took me to school on Grandfather's Day. I stood there beside him as he told three classes of students all about me.

Now we come to James and Hugh, aged 10 and 7, my youngest daughter's sons. They live on the Central Coast so we do not see them as much as we would like. Nor am I able to play with them, as I did the others. Age is such a barrier. However they enjoy soccer and teasing me about Rugby League. Set on the wrong track by their father, James and Hugh barrack for South Sydney. Last season, I must confess, I did a terrible thing — I barracked for the Rabbitohs just to please them!

OUR FINAL change of ownership proudly brought back the name Grace Gibson Radio Productions, and so it remains. When the Alberts decided to divest themselves of their broadcasting interests, they sold what was left of us in 1991 to one of my great unsung heroes —Bruce Ferrier.

Bruce's company, Independent Radio Services, specialised in Australian comedy, the genre we had never cracked. His iconic comedy series *How Green Was My Cactus* has actually overtaken the ABC's *Blue Hills* as Australia's longest radio feature in continuous production.

Bruce has great depth in radio; he understands the medium. In the late 1970s he headed 2GB/Macquarie's Special Events service, converting it into a programme feature producer harnessing big name presenters such as Dr James Wright, Bruce Bond, and David Koch, and producing comedies such as *The Boys from Benalla*.

Before he bought us from Alberts, Bruce had talked to me. I agreed we would be a good fit, the perfect merge of comedy and drama, and I promised to stay on if he bought it. The first thing he did was to revive the name Grace Gibson Radio Productions. Two weeks after Bruce took over, I had a bypass operation. It was time to slow down. Mostly now I act as a consultant, and advise clients which shows to choose from the old library. Even today, Grace's greatest serials — *Dossier on Dumetrius*, *Cattleman*, and *The Castlereagh Line* — are still being broadcast and enjoyed in Australia and overseas.

Bruce also added a new dimension to the company. Many of Grace's most popular shows are now available on CD for private listening. The list is amazing! Bruce invites all lovers of radio drama to purchase personal copies of their favourite shows from the Grace Gibson Radio Shop. Telephone **02 9906 2244**, write to PO Box 7377, Leura NSW, 2780, or log onto http://www.gracegibsonradio.com

HAPPILY, after 70 years, we have never been off the air. Somewhere, one of Grace's shows is playing. So please allow me as the oldest "cast member" to offer a few final reflections.

Grace believed that the broadcasting authorities should have set a small quota for stations to play Australian-produced radio drama. She felt that a lot of people who used to listen to radio had given it away.

Personally, I am in two minds about quotas. I have always resisted attempts to "force" people to listen to drama; for example, when Alberts tried to convert their Brisbane station to a drama outlet. I believe the old maxim about books still applies: *People read what they want to read.*

Well, it's the same with radio. People listen to what they want to hear. *The Castlereagh Line* is proof of that. So is *Yes, What?, Dad and Dave*, and *How Green Was My Cactus*. If quotas help leverage stations to give modern, entertaining, well-crafted drama a chance, fine. But they should never be used to force audiences to listen to it. And remember, some pretty awful films were made in years gone by when quotas were imposed on cinemas.

After television's arrival, radio obviously needed music and the immediacy of news. Then, talkback came and stayed. But — like drama — music, news, and talk had always been a feature of radio. There were talk shows on air back in the 1930s, and quiz shows still exist today as attractions to listeners. There were also cooking shows, variety shows, and vocal competitions such as *Australia's Amateur Hour* and *Mobil Quest*.

I suppose radio had to follow the lead of the United States and its supposed gurus, with ratings surveys whose results were always doubted except by the winners. Advertising agencies came into their own, attracted by the so-called statistics. Yet in the 1970s, 2UE Sydney was the leading radio station in Australia. Its morning magazine programme featured a variety of different segments — including 4-minute dramas and capsule features. It also starred Bob Rogers, who still works on Sydney radio after about 50 years.

HAVING just mentioned *Yes, What?*, I must pay tribute to that immortal programme! Perhaps I am still a boy at heart, but to me it was the funniest comedy ever broadcast on Australian radio. *Yes, What?*, also known as *Fourth Form at St Percy's*, hailed from the studios of 5AD Adelaide. It followed the escapades of schoolboys Greenbottle, Bottomly, and their classmates as they harassed schoolmaster Dr Pym. Rex "Wacka" Dawe scripted the show and starred as the hapless Pym. One of the young cast members, Ralph Peterson, went on to create the classic television comedy *My Name's McGooley, What's Yours?*

Starting in 1936, 520 episodes — or should I say lessons? — were recorded until the show had to stop when the cast signed up for War service. Sadly, one of the "boys" — Richard Harding-Browne — joined the RAAF and was killed over Europe in January 1942.

The story of this fabulous show is told in the book *Yes, What?* by Bob Hawker and Vern Sandfors. It is a great read. Eighty years after it was produced, *Yes, What?* is still being played on air and is now available on CD from the Grace Gibson Radio Shop. Just give Bruce Ferrier a call.

SO MUCH of my life has been tied up with the Australian Record Company. So many of our shows were recorded in their studios, and ARC pressed all our transcription discs. I have many memories and enduring friendships from those days. Terry O'Keefe and Alan Flannery, with whom I went to school, ran the transcription department. Alan went into insurance later and the first thing he did was try to sell me a policy! Terry and I are still in contact and meet up regularly; I was a groomsman at his wedding. Bill Denison is another friend whom I still see. He went from the transcription department to the factory where the records were made. Bob Corcoran was, of course, my best man, and his boss, Eric Cleeburn, was chief engineer and, so I am told, a difficult man to work with.

I have sung the praises of panel operators before. Now it is time to do so again. The brilliant Ron Wenban and Rod Tremaine were ARC's top studio panel operators. Their skills were exceptional. Spinning turntables, cueing the next discs, opening and closing faders, signalling to actors in the studios, and all the time maintaining an ear for quality and timing each show — I do not think an octopus could have accomplished what they did, and they did it with only one pair of hands! Rod was one of my favourite people. Every Friday he borrowed two pounds from me, paid it back the next Thursday, only to borrow it again on the Friday! These days, of course, panel operators are called sound engineers. Frankly, despite all their technical equipment, they would not survive if they had to contend with the problems of the 1940s and 1950s. I remember taking a visiting station manager to the 2UW control room, in the days when Alberts owned us. The sound engineer let us hear a 60-second commercial he had just completed. It was very good, but had taken five hours to prepare. We were amazed. In the good old days, it would have taken 20–30 minutes!

Formerly an engineer at British Australian Programmes, Bern Frost joined ARC and eventually went on to manage the recording factory. Not to be forgotten is young Mel Mayer who started as an office boy and ended up staying through all the corporate changes; he finally served as the archivist for the early days of ARC, Sony Music, and the other record labels. Also on the staff was Brian Westwood, the assistant to director Gordon Grimsdale. Brian later won two Archibald Prizes for portraits. Looking at his paintings I was not impressed — however Brian thought I was a Philistine!

As I have described earlier, ARC was on the third floor of Savoy House, and the light well was between my office and the ARC control room. One of the panel operators, who shall remain nameless, played a record of Doris Day singing *Que Sera Sera* all day. He would not stop. In the end, all I could do was to go upstairs and smash it.

Well, whatever will be, will be ...

WHICH brings me to the subject of my relationship with John Woodward, ARC's senior panel operator who later joined Grace's staff. John and I were not "friends" or "mates". If the truth be known, I think we barely "tolerated" each other. We both had tempers, and our day-to-day relations varied from frosty to stormy. Ever since John tried to "dob" in Ross Napier and me for having a few drinks, I had never felt comfortable with him. I also remember attending ARC's Christmas party one year and John made it very clear that he objected to my using the printing address machine and taking away all the second-hand packing. He could not do much about it, and I think that was what irked him. When Grace announced he was joining the staff as engineer in our new studio, I was immediately concerned. I went to see her and asked what my position would be in regard to John. She said he would have no authority over me. If she had said he was going to be senior to me, I am sure I would have resigned.

John used to boast that he once handed his resignation to Grace but she would not accept it. I stated that if he ever did that to me, I would indeed accept it.

I also suspected that John's commitment to quality was not what it should have been. The sound quality of *The Castlereagh Line* was not the only case in point. When the Alberts owned us, we were under pressure to perform profitably. We had been contracted to do all the dubbing work for Keith Graham's Seven Hills Productions; its office was only one hundred metres up the street, and I envisaged this job might lead to other work. John was obviously responsible for the quality control. At first there were some minor problems with dubs, but just when everything was going well, disaster struck in spades. Back came a week's supply of dubs. Further investigation showed that the recording turntable had not been on a flat surface. This was kindergarten stuff. I was furious and let John know about it. He responded by saying that he took every care but no responsibility. That made me even madder. I was determined that on this occasion he *would* take responsibility, and told him so. I went downstairs to cool off. When I returned to my office, John's resignation was on my desk; he refused to accept blame and consequently decided to quit. I left his resignation there for twenty-four hours in case he wanted to take it back. He did not, so I went in and told him it was accepted and when did he want to finish. I found out later that he had telephoned Grace to complain. We arranged a farewell lunch for him — which he did not like anyway — and, apart from Grace's funeral, that was the last I saw of him.

THE National Library of Australia commissioned Peter Burgis to obtain all the transcription discs stored away by radio production companies and commercial stations. The Library's plan was to store them in a special central facility in Canberra. Many old discs had already been lost, and it was a race against time to preserve our industry for study by future generations. Although Peter is no longer associated with the Archives, I believe he should be remembered for his achievement in ensuring that Australian radio drama is being preserved.

Although commercial radio drama had lasted only a relatively short time, it had a profound impact on the population — not just here, but throughout the English-speaking world. In fact it is still enjoyed by thousands of radio listeners today. Our final major serial, *The Castlereagh Line*, produced in the 1980s, has proved our most successful show ever. In 2015 it continues to be broadcast across Australia.

Grace Gibson's was the first company to give not only its stored transcriptions to the National Library's archives, but also its scripts, cost sheets, synopses, publicity material, and photographs. The only proviso was that if ever we needed access to a particular disc it would be made available. (After all, we were still selling shows and occasionally needed access to the odd missing episode.) Later, in the early 2000s, we arranged for the Archive to be given the 2WS compact disc library.

In 1984, the National Film and Sound Archive took over the collection. The first CEO was an Italian–American who seemed to speak very little English. I went down to Canberra for a week to meet the executives and staff. Some of the original staff from National Library days were still there, as friendly and helpful as ever. One of the tasks I undertook was cataloguing the photo files, supplying names to the faces.

A new CEO, Michael Loebenstein, took the reins in 2011. Bruce Ferrier and I met him, along with one of his executives Matthew who noted, "Before I retire my main aim is to arrange a formal agreement with Grace Gibson Productions."

The monumental task of cleaning and storing all our transcriptions has been completed. Scripts and programmes are now available for study and shortly we expect an arrangement will be finalised with NFSA that will prove very worthwhile.

The National Library's original vision has shown enormous foresight, preserving the work of our nation's actors, writers, producers, and technicians who developed a vital industry equal to anything in the world. Treasure it!

After all, as George Orwell wrote, "The most effective way to destroy people is to deny and obliterate their own understanding of their history." Amen to that.

I CANNOT recall who first started calling me "Uncle Reg". It may have been Bruce Carr at 4RO Rockhamton; we were great friends for a long time. Anyway it stuck, and I accepted it as a very friendly gesture and a sign that I was accepted into a very special group of young broadcasters. Even now I receive calls and messages from associates from long gone days. They bring back wonderful memories.

Today, one of my great joys is being asked to speak about the Golden Days to various groups of older people. Their faces really light up when they remember the programmes of long ago. At a recent talk I mentioned the 1930s serial *Inspector Scott of Scotland Yard* starring George Edwards. Afterwards, an elderly man came up to me and said, "Good shot, Inspector" and "Take him away", two of the inspector's catchphrases. He had been a devoted fan of the old show and we were basically the same age.

SINCE I have started writing this book, a number of radio friends have passed away: on the management side, Des Foster, a wonderful leader of the industry; James Condon, a top radio actor; Harry Griffiths, "Young Harry" from Roy Rene Mo's McCackie Mansions, the most listened to 12 minutes of comedy in Australian radio history; painter, playwright, and poet Rod Milgate, husband of Dinah Shearing; the acclaimed Australian actress Joan Lord — we were in the same church choir when I was a boy; Peter Benardos, the top radio panel operator and a pioneering television director; and of course the famous Aussie actor Rod Taylor. I trust I have not missed anyone; there are not that many left.

There are still a few of us around who wish to keep the great days of Australian radio alive. Bruce Ferrier and I are a keen combination, and Jim Aitchison is proving a great help. I only wish the commercial radio industry was interested. It may discover there is a lot more to radio than angry, disgruntled personalities, music that attracts limited age groups, repetitive newsbreaks, et cetera, et cetera. Gone, it seems, are the days when listeners were important. Today, as long as they get numbers in a survey book, who cares?

ON A NUMBER of occasions I have been asked about the value of our annual sales. The simple answer is, I have no idea.

It was not my concern and was purely Grace's business. My task was to help develop and market our new shows, maintain sales of all our shows, and keep things running smoothly. I had no part in the technical side either. Grace, with the help of her accountant, looked after the financial side. It was a struggle in the early years, and it was a struggle again in the 1960s and 1970s, but I am sure that the company was never in the red. She was also well in control of her personal financial position which was very strong. A newspaper once reported that Grace was the richest woman in Sydney. She responded by naming another woman and said, "She has more money than I do!"

In later years, I was sometimes asked if *I* was Grace Gibson's. My immediate reply was, "No!" I think that misunderstanding occurred because Grace kept a very low profile from the mid-1960s. The new generation of station managements did not know her personally; in fact, most had never even met or seen her. Nevertheless, the name of Grace Gibson Radio Productions was well respected throughout the broadcasting world, and I was assured of a welcome wherever I visited. Grace never lost interest in the company and, after I became sales manager in 1962, she gave me a free hand. But make no mistake, Grace was the boss until the day she retired, and even after that she would often ring me and give me advice. And until the end she had the final say over our new productions. As I was once quoted as saying, "The good Lord will only take Grace if He wants the place reorganised!"

I was very lucky at Grace Gibson's because after starting there at 16, I became the "everything person". I progressed through the various departments and was given every opportunity to learn more about the business. I was always included in auditions of new talent and anything else I wanted to do. I guess I became Grace's direct assistant — her right-hand man. If there was nobody else to do it, Grace always said, "Ask Reg James." It seems almost funny that for my entire business life I worked for a woman, but it never concerned me at all. I suppose my life *has* been dominated by strong women ... apart from Grace there was my mother, and then Neryl. So I was used to being "handled" by strong women and it did not matter to me a bit. God bless 'em, I say.

It certainly did not matter to Grace that she was a woman. Nobody told her that it was difficult for a woman to succeed in business. She just did it.

Acknowledgements

My sincere thanks to the new Grace Gibson team, Bruce and Robyn, who spent hours interviewing me and compiling transcripts of all my comments and memories.

It was only because of the enthusiasm of my co-author Jim that this book has been completed. His wish to edit and prepare it for printing has made my dream come true.

My heartfelt thanks to Commercial Radio Australia, who granted us permission to reproduce many historical photographs from their booklet *Let's Look at Radio*, published in the 1940s.

To Neryl, a big "thank you" for manning the computers and helping get this book ready. Now it's done, we can relax a little and you can show me all the work that needs doing in the garden!

Addendum
The Final Chapter
by Megan Hutchins

AS WE ALL stood around Dad's bedside early afternoon, toasting him and his life with a nip of whiskey, he said that he wished he could have added a final chapter to his book — his final hours with us all. To him it was the best way to pass; he couldn't quite believe his luck. I promised him that I would write the last chapter for him.

We were there when the ICU doctor got down on his knees and said, "Reg, the antibiotics are not working, the oxygen is not helping, your body is too weak. I suggest we take you off everything and let your body decide what it wants to do. Once your breathing becomes too difficult, we can give you morphine to make you more comfortable."

Dad said he was good with that; he didn't want morphine until he had seen all his children and grandchildren.

The doctor was so kind and beautiful with Dad. He said at this point it was all about respect and dignity. He said he was amazed by Dad's fortitude, the fact he was still alive, and that he seemed totally at peace and ready to go. The nursing staff at the San ICU were amazing; they kept out of the way and let us come in and out all afternoon and evening.

Everybody made it in time to see Dad, and he had a special message for all his children and grandchildren. He asked questions, just things on his mind and things he needed closure on, I'm guessing.

We told him we would not leave him, he would not be alone, and I instinctively gave touch as the only gift I could. We intuitively felt that he needed to feel safe and he did. The morphine process started; we knew the morphine was the beginning of the end, but it would be his friend.

He had a few doses of morphine to keep comfortable and then we cracked open the whiskey. We toasted my 50th Birthday, which he wasn't going to make. We toasted good health and safe travels, and we all laughed and made jokes. Mum held the glass and a straw, and he said this end couldn't be any better. I offered up another tipple and he said, "No thanks, Megs, I'm as high as a kite."

The grandchildren came back in and then it was like a domino effect, one lost it then the other, the other and the other. Dad then was openly weeping. To this day I still wonder if it was cruel to put him through that; however, he had good reason to cry as he was going to miss us all and not see his grandchildren grow up. As upsetting as it was, it was also quite beautiful.

The next few hours passed and Dad was in and out of his morphine state. If someone came in, he would be as alert as he could and would try to talk. He was truly amazing and one thing I realised, when he was in his final hours, was that he was a far stronger man than I ever thought. He was totally in control of his own passing, this was the way he wanted to farewell his family, embracing those final hours with us all.

We all took turns at sitting with him, and were all respectful of one another's need to have time alone.

Mum was with him in the afternoon and I saw looks between them that made me understand the love that has kept them married for over 50 years. An unbroken partnership focused on family.

Around 6.30 pm that night, Dad's vitals started to decline. We all came in again and stood around his bedside. At this stage he was breathing very slowly and was not communicating anymore. We watched the monitor and then focused our attention on just being with him in the moment as he passed away around thirty minutes later. He wasn't alone, he had human touch, he had his wife and family, and he had the perfect goodbye.

As for us, we had the perfect farewell, a closure that many are never blessed with.

All we have to do now is learn to live without our Dad and Papa, a truly remarkable and highly respected man right until the end.

www.ingramcontent.com/pod-product-compliance
Lightning Source LLC
Chambersburg PA
CBHW031313150426
43191CB00005B/214